THE WHIDDEN LECTURES FOR 1973

The
Nemesis of
Empire

E. T. SALMON

Messecar Professor of History,
McMaster University

LONDON
OXFORD UNIVERSITY PRESS
NEW YORK   TORONTO
1974

Oxford University Press, Ely House, London W. 1

GLASGOW NEW YORK TORONTO MELBOURNE WELLINGTON
CAPE TOWN IBADAN NAIROBI DAR ES SALAAM LUSAKA ADDIS ABABA
DELHI BOMBAY CALCUTTA MADRAS KARACHI LAHORE DACCA
KUALA LUMPUR SINGAPORE HONG KONG TOKYO

ISBN 0 19 211620 7

© Oxford University Press 1974

PRINTED IN GREAT BRITAIN BY
THE CAMELOT PRESS LTD, SOUTHAMPTON

Foreword

The Whidden Lectures derive from the benefice of the late E. Carey Fox, B.A., LL.D., a graduate of McMaster University during its Toronto days, later the senior member of the Board of Governors and Chancellor of the University. The lectures were established to honour the memory of the Reverend Howard Primrose Whidden, D.D., LL.D., D.C.L., F.R.S.C. (1871–1952), the chief executive officer of the University from 1923 to 1941. The lectures were meant to introduce scholars who would help students to cross the barriers between the academic departments of a modern university. There was no restriction as to general theme.

Dr. Whidden was born into a family resident since 1761 in Antigonish, Nova Scotia. Educated at Acadia University in Wolfville, Nova Scotia, at McMaster University, and at the Univeristy of Chicago, Dr. Whidden subsequently served as Baptist Minister in Ontario, Manitoba, and Ohio. He was President of Brandon College during its affiliation with McMaster University from 1913 to 1923 and served as Union Government member for Brandon in the House of Commons in Ottawa from 1917 to 1921. Dr. Whidden and his close friend, Dr. Fox, with uncommon vision and courage executed the transfer of the University from Toronto, its home since 1887, to Hamilton in 1930. Dr. Whidden ranks as the University's second Romulus; Dr. Fox commands respect as the University's egregious benefactor.

The eighteenth series of lectures was delivered in January 1973 by Edward Togo Salmon, M.A., Ph.D., D.Litt., LL.D., F.R.S.C., F.R.H.S., F.B.A., Messecar Professor of History and University Orator in McMaster University. His topic, *The Nemesis of Empire*, is one of perennial concern to historians and of immediate concern to everyone who has witnessed the decline and dissolution of the British Empire.

Born in England and raised in Australia, Dr. Salmon obtained his classical education in Sydney and in Cambridge, England. After brief service at Acadia University, Dr. Salmon came to McMaster in 1930 to join the Department of Classics and later the Department of History. His energies and capacities soon became manifest not only in his scholarly career, his important publications, and his service to classical organizations at home and abroad, but also in his role as departmental and administrative officer.

His career as Principal of University College during the emotional 'sixties (1961–7) and as First Vice-President of the newly established Division of Arts (1967–8) is memorialized by curricular innovations and by the splendid buildings of the Arts Complex. Few professors have contributed so richly and so decisively to the advancement of the University's distinction and international stature.

Dr. Salmon has been President of the Classical Association of Canada (1952–4), Member of the Executive Committee of the International Federation of Classical Associations (1959–69), Member of the Humanities Research Council of Canada (1965–8), President of the American Philological Association (1971), and Vice-President of the International Council for Philosophy and Humanistic Sciences, a sub-agency of U.N.E.S.C.O., since 1971.

His many administrative roles and public service in no way diminished his productivity as scholar. His *History of the Roman World, 30 B.C.–A.D. 138* has entered upon its sixth edition (1968); his *Samnium and the Samnites* (1967) won the coveted Merit Award of the American Philological Association; his *Roman Colonization Under the Republic* (1969) was the product of years of topographical and historical research throughout the length and breadth of Italy.

Elections to Learned Societies have brought distinction to the man and to his University: Fellow, Royal Society of Canada; Fellow, Royal Historical Society; Honorary Member, Australian Classical Society; Honorary Member, Society for the Promotion of Roman Studies; Fellow of the Canadian Institute in Rome; and, most notably, Corresponding Fellow of the British Academy (1971).

Dr. Salmon ranks as McMaster's most distinguished humanist. Visiting Lectureships in Australia, the

United Kingdom, Eire, and the United States and his recent Professorship at the Intercollegiate Centre for Classical Studies in Rome (1969–71) have won international respect for his wisdom and scholarship.

The members of the audience who attended his Whidden Lectures were captivated by his distinctive style, by the breadth of his erudition, and by the grace of his oratory. A larger company of his students, many of whom have digressed widely from the Groves of Academe, will recall past lectures, genial words of friendship, and the warmth of his personality when they read this published version. Dr. Salmon is the first member of the McMaster University Faculty to appear as Whidden Lecturer. The Selection Committee thereby honoured the first chairman of the Whidden Lectures Committee and introduced to a capacity audience one of McMaster's most distinguished statesmen and teachers and one of her most zealous servants.

McMaster University   A. G. McKay

Contents

I

'A Fit of Absence of Mind'

Britain's forward step into Europe makes timely a backward glance at her empire. It was often viewed by its advocates as an advanced analogy to the Roman Empire. Both imperial powers had expanded initially without premeditation, programmes, or policies; both had faced acute crises of inadequate government and had renewed their lease of life to become supreme powers.

But besides these superficial coincidences the Roman and the British empires are very unlike in their manner of birth and growth and show significant contrasts which underline their whole history.

Will you let me begin on a very personal note? It is an exceptional honour to be invited to deliver the Whidden Lectures. The many distinguished scholars who have appeared in the series in the past have won for it an enviable reputation, and to be thought worthy of inclusion in their company is a compliment indeed. Nor am I unappreciative of the fact that, although other Canadian scholars have been Whidden Lecturers before me, I belong to McMaster itself. I hope that I shall be easily understood, even though I cannot find the words to tell you how proud this makes me.

But I have yet another and a much better reason for being grateful to the Whidden Lectures committee.

Unlike all those who have appeared before me on this platform, I was acquainted, and indeed well acquainted, with Dr. Whidden; and not only with Dr. Whidden, but also with Dr. Fox, that great friend of McMaster whose generosity twenty years ago made this lecture series possible. I had much affection and unbounded admiration for these two great Canadians, and I am deeply thankful that I have been given an opportunity to pay what tribute I can to their memory. To that end I have chosen a theme that would have been dear to the heart of Howard Whidden: he came of British Empire loyalist stock, as did his wife. And I have endeavoured to treat the theme in a manner of which Carey Fox would have approved; his desire always was to have different specialities and disciplines brought more closely together. I have accordingly tried to confront the British with the Romans. The subject is made topical by the New Year's Day entry into Europe's Common Market of the British, who have thereby opened up a new chapter in their long history, turning their backs on their imperial past.

Those of us who were born in Edwardian times have been privileged to witness not only the finest hour, but also the greatest days, of the British Empire. By 1920 the supremacy of the Royal Navy, repelling the challenge of Kaiser Wilhelm's fleet in the wasteful 'dreadnought' race, had triumphantly reasserted itself. Great Britain and the Empire had not only fought the war that was to end all wars and make a world fit for heroes to live in, but had also emerged from that bloodiest of all conflicts unbowed, victorious, and enlarged. Those who were schoolchildren in those heady days will remember the excitement of Empire Day festivities. The ritual of the celebrations in the school that I attended did not vary greatly from one year to the next. On the eve of the Empire Day holiday, there would be a general assembly of all the students, featured by a stirring recitation of appropriate verses from Rudyard Kipling, followed by a wheezy gramophone recording of Dame Clara Butt singing Elgar's 'Land of Hope and Glory'; all present would then raise their voices in unison to the spirited strains of 'Rule, Britannia' and, after some speechifying and flag-waving, would wend their homeward way, proud, exhilarated, and uplifted, to let off fire-crackers around a bonfire in the evening.

In retrospect, half a century later, it all seems completely remote, if not more than a little incredible. It was another world, a world of ebullient chauvinism from which we have since shaken loose to move into the emancipated if somewhat bewildering days of the second half of the twentieth century, when the British Empire has become one with the snows of yesteryear and when uncertainty reigns as to what will replace it as the rock of stability for a wobbling world.

In 1914 Great Britain and her overseas dependencies formed some sort of imperial unity. The declaration of war by Britain on the 4th of August in that year bound the whole of it, and the members of the Empire marched shoulder to shoulder against the Central Powers. In World War II a mere quarter of a century

3

later, they once again marched together, but this time much more in the manner of a fighting alliance than of an organic union. Canada, for instance, made her own declaration of war, and she did not do it merely in tame imitation of Britain, nor even at precisely the same moment. Officially, Canada was at war with Japan before Britain was (or, for that matter, even before the U.S.A. was), and officially she was never at war with Bulgaria at all. Nevertheless there can be no doubt that in World War II the imperial connection still counted for much.

It seems hardly likely that this will ever be the case again. No one believes that there could be similar concerted action in the unthinkable event of the world being subjected to the horror of a third world war. By 1970, another bare twenty-five years later, the various countries of the Empire had decided to go their separate ways, with some of them no longer recognizing even the tenuous link of the British crown. True, most of them have agreed to continue in close consultation, and even to practise a certain amount of co-operation, with one another in the Commonwealth. But this does not disguise the reality that their feet have been swiftly and firmly planted upon different paths, even upon paths that in one or two instances have already led them into war with one another.

The rapidity with which the British Empire has crumbled seems all the more startling in that this has occurred so soon after it had reached its furthest territorial extension. The days immediately after

4

World War I saw it at its zenith. It was in the halcyon days of the early twenties that Cecil Rhodes's imperial dream of an all-red route from the Cape to Cairo was translated, if only briefly, into reality; and as its inhabitants of the time were so fond of repeating, the Empire had become the mighty organism spread over one-quarter of the world's surface on which the sun never set.

But by definition every zenith is the start of a decline. Already, during World War I, the Empire had sometimes been unofficially referred to as the British Commonwealth of Nations, and in 1922 this expression was actually used in an official document of the very highest importance.[1] At the imperial conference in 1926, the Balfour Declaration attempted to define the concept, and the definition was published and even spelled out in some detail in the Statute of Westminster in 1931. The British Empire thus became the British Commonwealth; and not many years were to elapse before the adjective British had disappeared from the title, and nothing remained of the British Empire other than a handful of islands scattered here and there over the world's oceans.

So remarkable a reversal has inevitably opened the floodgates to a veritable spate of interpretations, explanations, and conjectures. In recent years particularly, much has been written about the end of the British Empire.[2] My hardihood in taking up the theme yet again is due not only to the interest which a 'decline and fall' is bound to arouse in a Roman historian, but also to the hope that a look at the British Empire in the light of the Roman experience may well prove illuminating.

I hasten to add that this implies no suggestion that I find history to be self-repeating. The theory that it is remains unconvincing despite an erudite and novel restatement of it by A. J. Toynbee. H. A. L. Fisher himself could not discover in history 'a plot, a rhythm, a predestined pattern'.[3] Most of us recognize, with Fisher, the part played by pure chance and blind coincidence in the affairs of men, and agree with Walpole that history does not repeat itself no matter how much historians may repeat one another. Mommsen, the greatest modern student of ancient Rome, insisted that men's actions are only too often governed by passion rather than by reason; and passion is too unpredictable to conform to any pattern.

Analogies, however, do obviously exist between the Roman and the British imperial histories. In fact, of all the earlier empires, the Roman is the only one that is even remotely similar to the British in extension, variety, and duration, although one should add that it was also markedly different in many ways. The Romans, too, encompassed much of the world of their time; and their regime, like that of the British, was featured by a long period of peace on the world-wide scale, actually the longest in history. Indeed, Rome served as an inspiration and even to some extent as a model for the British, especially at the time when the latter became imbued with the concept of imperial purpose.

6

If it is a matter of interest to us to understand what happened to the Empire of which we so recently formed a part, its evolution will be seen more clearly perhaps when compared and contrasted with that of its Roman forerunner.

The starting point for the two imperial expansions is one of difference: in time, in historical background, and in circumstance. Rome had to fight for survival against strong rivals, even inside Italy. Defeat in her early struggles would have meant subjection, and for her the only alternative was supremacy. The Samnite and the Punic Wars had steeled Roman tenacity and self-discipline to the utmost. After the fall of Carthage there were no equal rivals for dominion, although even yet there were many reversals in both internal and external matters still to come. The Roman senate, effectively the government of the Roman Republic, was fully involved from the outset.

Contrast England. England's, and later Great Britain's, expansion originated from private enterprise, with trading posts and with settlements that were barely official. The competition with Spain, with Portugal, with Holland and, above all, with France put much wind into the sails of the companies of Merchant Adventurers, as well as into those of the Royal Navy. But, apart from the crown patents and charters accorded the companies, there was at first not much real commitment by the government.

Besides contrasts, however, there are broad coincidences. Both Rome and the British imperial power grew without premeditation, programme, or policy, and merely as events dictated, the Romans mostly for strategic reasons, the British mostly out of the necessity to trade. This haphazard opportunism was followed for a long time in both cases by inadequate administration of the annexed territories. Ultimately the problems and crises of the first phase of development in each of the two empires were solved, in the Roman world by the reforms of the emperor Augustus shortly before the birth of Christ, and in the British by the effects of the great changes in the social and political spheres and by the rise in moral and humanitarian standards that bred a sense of imperial mission in the nineteenth century.

In the case of any empire there will probably be some difficulty in pinpointing the precise date of its earliest beginnings. It has sometimes been implied that the Roman Empire began when Rome, the city republic on the River Tiber, brought the whole of Italy under her control between the fifth and the third centuries B.C. This, however, seems very doubtful. It is something like saying that the start of the British Empire is to be sought in the achievement of the kingdom of Wessex in suppressing the independent existence of the other Anglo-Saxon realms that disputed the soil of England with it. It is, of course, true that the supremacy established by Rome in Italy before 100 B.C. was very different, both in legal theory and in actual fact, from the unification imposed by Wessex on the England of the heptarchy before A.D. 1000. Nevertheless, neither the one nor the other accomplishment can really be considered imperial expansion. It is conceding but little to the salt water fallacy to subscribe to the usual opinion that, in the case of both Rome and England, empire began with the annexation of territories overseas, provinces in the case of the Romans, colonies in the case of the English.

When, shortly after 300 B.C., Rome had established her hegemony in Italy, she put an end to the cherished and immemorial habit of the Italic peoples of going to war with one another, and she obliged them to expend their martial energies in another way, namely in helping her to defend Italy, and what she considered to be the interests of Italy, against external attack. But she did not demand taxes or tribute from the Italians, she did not impose her laws or her language upon them, and she did not annex, much less annihilate them: technically they were her allies. It was not until 90 B.C., by which time many of the Italians had adopted Latin and Rome's ways, that they were incorporated into the Roman state. And when that finally happened they were brought in, not as subjects but as Roman citizens. In Italy Rome had unified a nation, not created an empire.

But, even before 90 B.C., the Roman Empire had already begun, in the third century B.C. in fact, when Rome annexed Sicily after the victory which she and her Italian allies had won over Carthage in the First Punic War. Out of the Sicilian acorn grew the mighty oak-tree, which we call the Roman Empire and which was to sink its roots so deep that countries like France,

Spain, Portugal, Switzerland, and Romania still speak the language of the Romans in one or other of its Neo-Latin forms. It spread its branches all over the Mediterranean world and the present-day Middle East and North Africa, over central and western Europe, and even over Britain. And it cast its shadow still further afield, as far as India and Central Asia.

For the Romans the annexation of Sicily in the third century B.C. was an act of prudential self-defence. The Carthaginians had penetrated into the island in force and thus posed a threat to mainland Italy; and there was even the very real risk that they would allow none but their own ships to sail through the narrow straits that on the one side separate Sicily from mainland Italy and on the other divide Sicily from North Africa. To put an end to this menace, the Romans forcibly ejected the Carthaginians from the island and, to make sure that they never came back, annexed it themselves. Sicily thus became the first segment of the Roman Empire, Rome's first province.

It was once again for reasons of defence that Rome decided on possession of parts of Spain, about the year 200 B.C. Her object was to deny the Iberian peninsula as a base to any would-be aggressor against Italy. The Romans were hardly likely to forget that Hannibal the Carthaginian had mounted his assault on Italy from there.

Still later in the second century B.C., it was once more the need for security, real or fancied, that caused the Romans to consolidate their power on the other side of the Adriatic, in the lands now occupied by Yugoslavia, Albania, and Greece.

At no time in their history were the Romans prepared to tolerate a strong large power as their nearest neighbour, if they could possibly prevent it. Accordingly they sought to establish across the Adriatic a system of small states, no single one of which would be strong enough to bring the others under its control and thus become a potential threat to Italy. The British preoccupation that no power in Europe should become a threat to Britain and her cross-channel policy of preventing such a threat come to mind. The Romans actually set up a balanced system of trans-Adriatic states in 196 B.C., and for the next half century they went to considerable effort and trouble to maintain it. Ultimately, however, they had to concede that the preponderance of the state of Macedon was such that it was bound to upset any balance of power immediately east of the Adriatic; and it was then, in 146 B.C., that the Romans first resorted to annexation in that area and got their first possessions in the Greek-speaking eastern end of the Mediterranean. It hardly looks like premeditated aggression.

Indeed it is not difficult to demonstrate that the Roman senate (and it was the senate that decided policy under the Roman Republic) was anything but eager to embark on wars of conquest.[4] The priestly law of Rome forbade wars of aggression in any case and, besides, it was undesirable for her to become responsible for the direct administration of territories beyond the seas. Therefore, in the senate's view, additional commitments were generally to be avoided: they should be accepted only if they contributed to the defence of Italy. Even when Hellenistic monarchs bequeathed their kingdoms to Rome, as they occasionally did in the second and first centuries B.C., vaguely in the same way that Edward the Confessor is reported to have left England by testamentary disposition to William the Conqueror, the Roman senate did not invariably take up the legacy, even though it would have meant acquiring empire without effort. In 96 B.C. the senate avoided taking Cyrene at the first time of asking; and in 88 B.C. again it refused to accept Egypt, potentially a most valuable acquisition, when one of the Ptolemies offered that kingdom to Rome in his will. (Both countries did become Roman later.)

On the other hand, the Romans were prepared to accept such bequests of kingdoms whenever they thought it in their interest to do so: they obtained Pergamum in this way in 134 B.C. and Bithynia in 74 B.C. They, of course, also showed little hesitation in seizing territories by conquest, whenever they felt that this was necessary in defence of their own security.

A defensive war is admittedly a highly subjective and very elastic concept, and it would be naïve to think that there were not often other and unavowed motives mixed up with the Romans' concern, genuine or feigned, for their own security. To serve their personal ambition, powerful individuals sometimes transgressed official policy. Roman commanders were capable of gratuitously attacking some backward tribe, in the certain knowledge that no government will determinedly discipline or readily repudiate a striking military success, even one achieved against orders; and Roman generals hungered for military success, even if cheaply won over primitive peoples, since it paved the way to the celebration of a triumph, that gorgeous processional spectacle which ensured a man's political future and, in the poet Horace's words, for a giddy moment made him the veritable equal of the gods.

Once Rome had become mighty, the temptation to use her power was overwhelming, always of course in the ostensible interests of her own security. Even the gentle Virgil, in the last century before Christ, proclaimed it Rome's duty to humble the proud in defensive wars;[5] and, a hundred years later, the Elder Pliny seems to have taken it casually for granted that Rome's mission should be to continue expanding her world empire and enforce a Roman peace.[6] Inevitably, therefore, the real reasons for annexations were only too liable to become mixed and murky. The Roman conquest of Britain in A.D. 43 is an instructive example. Officially it was another case of self-defence, an attempt to protect Roman possessions in Gaul against threats from across the Channel. But, in fact, it looks much more like a case of sheer aggression, possibly with the object of bolstering a precarious regime with a resounding military success abroad. Or it may even be that on this occasion there was an economic motive and that the Romans were attracted by the precious stones and the minerals with which the island was reputedly stuffed.

Economic motives, it must be admitted, do not seem to have normally affected Roman policy very much, even if they may have done so in the case of Britain. Usually it was not with some idea of acquiring markets or control of raw materials that Rome made additions to her Empire. Roman history cannot show anything really to parallel the kind of initiative allowed to the East India Company in Asia, the Company of Adventurers of London Trading into Africa, or the Hudson's Bay Company in Canada; and it follows that it also cannot show the sort of development that such initiative led to.

Nevertheless, economic considerations were by no means invariably ignored. The Romans were certainly not indifferent to the spoils of war or to the tribute that could be extracted from a subjugated people; and there might be other material gains, as well. Augustus' abortive attempt in 25 B.C. on the fabled land once ruled by the Queen of Sheba may have been due to a desire to obtain control of the desert caravan trade. Again, the Roman general, who informed a group of Gauls in A.D. 70, after a short-lived rebellion, that Rome had not gone into their country in the first place out of any desire for gain, sounds more disingenuous than convincing.[7] Furthermore, examples can be adduced of the Roman armed services being obliged to intervene when traders got into trouble in foreign parts. As early as the third century B.C. an army was sent across the Adriatic to protect Italian merchants who had ventured into today's Yugoslavia.

Nevertheless, despite many cases of unofficial and even of official abuses of power and of other forms of irresponsible behaviour, it is still the case that Rome did not pursue a policy of aggrandisement aiming at providing opportunities for enrichment in the first place. Her usual motive in annexing provinces was to strengthen her imperial defences. She was engaged on the search for secure, natural, and if possible impregnable frontiers and to that end carried her conquests forward to rivers, to mountain ranges, to deserts, and to sea-coasts.

The genesis of the British Empire, too, is to be sought in the annexation of transmarine territories. Traditionally it dates from 1583, the year when Sir Humphrey Gilbert laid claim to Newfoundland for the English crown; his expedition, however, ended up ineffectually, he himself being shipwrecked and losing his life. The real beginnings came a score or so of years later, with the establishment of the settlements in Virginia, and in particular the one at Jamestown in 1607.

But whereas it was a desire to feel secure that chiefly induced the Romans to annex areas and convert them into provinces, it was an eagerness to expand trade that acquired colonies for the English. In the first instance it was a competitive and enterprising search for trade routes to the Far East that took them into all parts of the Atlantic; and it led them into the venture that has come to be known as the first British Empire. In fact, in the case of the English, so predominant was the economic motive that with them trade, instead of following the flag as it is proverbially supposed to do, often preceded it.

The story of the earliest English colonies is a chronicle of private companies being authorized by royal charter to trade and, if need be, to found settlements and maintain armed forces in specified regions overseas, entirely at their own risk and at their own expense. The American colonies got their start in this way; and the beginnings of the Empire in India were not essentially different. The flag often did not arrive until somewhat later, when London decided to make the settlements thus brought into being the direct responsibility of the crown. Two of the thirteen north American colonies that fought Britain in the 1770s, Pennsylvania and Maryland, remained proprietary colonies almost down to the very outbreak of the War of Independence. Indeed, the flag sometimes took its time in arriving, the British government, like the Roman senate, being very reluctant to assume the additional commitments that enlargement of the Empire entailed. The Gambia and British Honduras had been British trading-posts for something like two hundred years before the British government showed much official interest in them. In their case relative obscurity and unhealthy climate might account for the neglect. But it is to be noted that considerable prodding of the London authorities was needed, before even so magnificent a country as New Zealand was officially pronounced British.

It can, of course, be readily admitted that in the case of the British, as of the Romans, other subsidiary reasons besides the principal one often played a part in the decision to make a colony. North Americans need no reminder that the flight from religious and other forms of persecution or that the compulsion the British felt themselves to be under to keep other powers out, such as the Spanish, the Portuguese, the Dutch, and the French, contributed to the birth of some colonies.

Especially in the growth of the so-called Second British Empire was the economic motive frequently combined with, and sometimes obscured by, other causes, a fact that enabled Sir John Seeley, late in the nineteenth century, to make his oft-quoted quip about the Empire seeming to have been acquired in a fit of absence of mind.[8]

Captain Cook went to the Pacific at the behest of the Royal Society as well as of the British admiralty: besides investigating and mapping the antipodean lands his task was to observe the transit of the planet Venus. And his successful accomplishment of both these missions did not so much open up a new area for trade, immediately anyway, as provide England with a dumping ground for her felons and gaolbirds.

Humanitarian zeal and religious fervour were also incentives. After 1807 Wilberforce's campaign against slavery and, later in the century, Dr. Livingstone's missionary explorations led to the enlargement of the Empire of Africa. Elsewhere, in places like Sarawak and Burma, a determination to free native peoples from tyrannical rulers or to terminate chaotic threats to international peace was the motive.

Strategic considerations also were often very much to the fore, needless to say: even Adam Smith, after all, allowed that 'defence is of much more importance than opulence'.[9] It was the need for military bases, provision points, and coaling stations to enable the Royal Navy, the Empire's instrument of power, to protect the route to India that brought places like Malta, Perim, and Aden under the Union Jack; and Britain's action in taking Cape Colony from the Dutch and Mauritius from the French after the Napoleonic wars was scarcely any different: it had the safeguarding of the Indian Ocean as its object.

Nevertheless, the thought of trade was always uppermost. Even where the British professed other reasons for their action, they were never entirely oblivious of the commercial prospects. In the Indian Ocean area for example, Stamford Raffles was eager to have Java as well as Mauritius annexed after the Napoleonic Wars, undoubtedly because of its economic possibilities, although his publicly announced reason was the desirability of liberating the Indonesians from what he described as the brutal and degrading rule of the Dutch. Fortunately no doubt for the reputation of perfidious Albion, Raffles's proposal was not carried out. He made up for it, however, by establishing Singapore as an entrepôt of trade; and, like Hong Kong, another island off the coast of Asia that became a British colony in the nineteenth century, Singapore has been amazingly successful in the role.

Even in the late Victorian age, when liberal

humanitarianism was very much in vogue, and nowhere more so than in the British Empire, the urge to annex colonies for purposes of trade was still very strong. The notorious 'scramble for Africa' was largely a race for materials, markets, and money, and men like Cecil Rhodes ensured that Britain was a leading contender. In a single ten-year period she added well over a million square miles to her African possessions, an area equivalent in size to one-third of all Europe.

It will be seen, then, that even though empire began for both the Romans and the British when they expanded out of home territory into areas overseas, the start, growth, and ultimate wide extension of the two dominions were due to markedly differing causes. In one respect at least, however, there was similarity: both the Romans and the British, in the early stages of their empire-building, behaved as if empire existed largely, if not wholly, for the benefit of the imperial power.

For many years the main concern of the Romans was to get what they could out of their empire without bothering to consider whether they owed it anything in return. They may not have acquired their provinces in the first place for the sake of trade or commerce, but once firmly in possession of them, they proceeded to exploit and plunder them. They clearly did not go so far as to kill the geese that were laying the golden eggs, but they did despoil their nests with ruthless regularity.

The quality of the officials that the Roman Republic sent to its provinces was often objectionable, or worse.

Some of its governors were avariciousness personified; and the natives they governed had no real safeguards against their cruelty or their methods of extortion, whether through local leading men in the provinces or through any other means. Gaius Gracchus in the second century B.C. made the revealing remark that wine-jars usually came back from the provinces filled with gold and silver;[10] and, a little later, a native of Dalmatia observed that the Romans did not send watchdogs or shepherds to guard their flocks, but ravening wolves.[11] Nor was the Dalmatian exaggerating. Cicero has left us a monumental picture of rapacity and viciousness in the person of Verres, the governor of Sicily, who plundered that province unconscionably in the first century B.C. Admittedly Cicero was speaking as legal counsel for some of Verres's victims and may have exaggerated his account to some extent. But it is significant that elsewhere, in a work that has nothing to do with the obnoxious Verres and his nefarious activities, Cicero again condemns the excesses of provincial administration under the Roman Republic. His actual words are: 'It is difficult to find words to express how fiercely we Romans are hated by the peoples of our Empire because of the wicked and wanton behaviour of the governors we have sent to them of recent years.'[12]

One instrument that could minister to a governor's greed was the armed force under his command. The Roman Republic of the days before Christ, remarkably enough, did not have a standing army. This is all the more surprising in view of the fact that the Romans, in marked contrast with the British, always made the army their instrument of power. The practice of the Roman Republic was to raise field forces if, as and when they were needed, conscripting Roman citizens for the purpose. As it happens, field forces were needed with sufficient frequency for there always to be some of them in being somewhere. Even so, a standing army was officially lacking and this made any methodical or continuous planning for garrisoning and defence purposes impossible. Instead, the Roman senate decided each year where to send troops and in what numbers. The system was far from ideal, for the senate might misjudge the need or, even worse, it might play politics and vote troops only for those provinces where it suited the personal interest of its most influential members to have them sent. But the system was made to order for any unscrupulous person who happened to be governor of a province in a year when troops were posted to it. For, in the absence of permanent army quarters, he billeted the troops in the towns of the province. There the behaviour of the conscripts was regularly so unbridled and outrageous that most communities were prepared to pay virtually unlimited sums to be exempted from the evil of having troops billeted on them; and many governors allowed themselves to be bribed by wealthy cities, the wealthier the better, into quartering the soldiers elsewhere.[13]

And the governors not only gouged their provinces. They also often failed in their elementary duty of defending them. In the last century B.C. provinces were liable to be overrun by invading enemies; and it was not entirely inadequate provision by the Roman senate that was responsible for this state of affairs. It was the governors who were chiefly to blame, since they were prone to devote more of their attention to plundering their charges than to protecting them.

Exploitation, moreover, was not confined to the ranks of the Roman officials. It was also practised, and on a massive scale, by private individuals, operating from positions of favour and advantage and working under the protection of officialdom.

There was a seemingly ineradicable and abiding tradition among the aristocrats who constituted the governing class in the Roman Republic that it was their prerogative and privilege to manipulate the public state machinery for their own ends. As a consequence, the Roman senate was frequently under pressure from private individuals or groups, who were seeking to influence public policy for their personal profit. Sometimes such groups actually succeeded in promoting their economic fortunes with the backing of Roman expeditionary forces. In the late second century B.C., for instance, a Roman tax-farming company was enabled to extend the range of its profit-making activities in Asia Minor.[14] And in the first century B.C. the future leader of the conspirators who assassinated Julius Caesar, the celebrated Brutus, Shakespeare's 'noblest Roman of them all', did not hesitate to use public means, that is Roman troops, in order to collect, brutally and callously, debts that were owed to him privately.

It is true that the Roman senate did not always tamely yield to such attempts at undue influence and sinister persuasion. Sometimes it sought to curb the greedy designs of Roman capitalists. In 167 B.C., for instance, it would not allow Roman corporations to lease the gold and silver mines of Macedon, giving two reasons for its refusal: first, the said contractors might oppress the natives, and secondly, they might build up private interests in Macedon too dangerous to contemplate.[15] But the slowness of communications and the long distances involved ran counter to any good intentions the senate may have had. It was a physical impossibility for it to supervise the provinces closely and continuously. The plain truth is that the administration of the provinces of the Roman Republic in the days before Christ was often deplorable and scandalous.

Moreover, the provinces suffered, like Rome herself, from the recurring crises of the last century of the Republic. These were the times of Sulla, of Pompey, and of Julius Caesar, when the whole Roman world was torn asunder by driving ambition and ruthless self-interest. The strongest and most sacred principles of government were threatened and Rome seemed about to fall apart. It was then that Augustus came, just in time to resolve a most dangerous crisis in the life of the Roman state; and he made it his task to restore the forces which had been the foundation of Roman life and government: he proceeded to revive respect for tradition and to extend Roman authority. Liberty was not revived. Ultimately, however, the application of Augustus' policies brought stability, peace, and the Roman civilization to the world.

This remarkable lease of life which Augustus succeeded in fashioning for the Roman Empire could, I suspect, have enheartened those British imperialists who, after the loss of the American colonies and the perils resulting therefrom, sought inspiration in Roman history. For down to 1776 the English colonies had been regarded largely as business arrangements, outlets for emigration, and sources of revenue. Most of them, as already noted, had been brought into being by private enterprise or religious dissent, not by acts of state; and this had given the colonists an independence of outlook that objected to the restrictive trading practices established by eighteenth-century England. They themselves did not seek to share in the life and government of the mother country, nor did England seek to attract them. In the eighteenth century, England pursued a mercantilist policy specifically designed to extract the maximum profit from her colonies. In Africa the British built up a virtual monopoly of the slave trade. In India there was rampant profiteering. Robert Clive's personal gains were admitted to amount to well over two million of today's dollars, and his calm announcement to an investigating committee of the House of Commons, 'I stand amazed at my own moderation', suggests that other nabobs were getting more. All this obscured whatever merits there may have been in the British administration of those days. The court of law that finally, after many years of litigation, acquitted Warren Hastings of lining his own pockets could hardly have denied that his activities in Bengal had been intended to further, first and foremost, the interests of Britain. The corruption and the abuses of the East India Company, through which the British wielded their power in India at that time, were so notorious that they were just as violently denounced as those of Verres had been by Cicero: the mildest description that the playwright Sheridan could find for the company's rapacious officials was that they were 'highwaymen in kid gloves'. One source of the company's wealth was the fabulous profits made by smuggling opium from India to China; and the British government shared in these profits by taxing them.

It was the sobering loss of the American colonies that first obliged British statesmen to take stock. Undoubtedly there was a consciousness of neglect in past British colonial administration, and to some it appeared inevitable that all the colonies were soon to be emancipated. Meanwhile, however, the rallying of the Empire loyalists to Canada and the increasing adherence to British administration in India proved that the life of the Empire was not at an end after all. Simultaneously in Britain itself extraordinary transformations were taking place: these were the effects of the industrial revolution, which changed the life and orientation of the middle class, and the just as remarkable moral revolution, which aroused a religious, evangelical, and humanitarian enthusiasm, that had actually begun some generations earlier but only now became a mounting force of enormous importance leading, amongst other things, to the abolition of the slave trade. Moreover, influences coming from egalitarian France and the more urgent tendencies to liberalism in Britain itself caused profound changes in government and in its sense of responsibility to the governed. Adopting these new ethical and political attitudes, the British nation sought to rationalize its behaviour and to ask itself whether what it was doing was either morally right or materially worthwhile.[16] And it was in that age of missionary zeal that there emerged a view of the purpose of empire that was often compared at the time to that of Rome. The British Empire, it was thought, would bring a new era of peace in which unity and good government would spread over the world as in the best years of the Pax Romana.

Not that Britain was geographically well situated for such a role. Whereas Rome, centrally placed in her Mediterranean and Continental empire, was able to maintain relatively easy intercommunication and exchange with her provinces and become a nucleus from which romanization could spontaneously radiate, Great Britain could not form a similar link with her colonies, separated as she was before the steamship era by several weeks of travel from the nearest of them. Only later, when the Royal Navy developed swifter connections and made Britain less remote, could her accumulated store of civilization be effectively transmitted. Interchange with countries of high culture, such as India, then grew much more active, although for Britain imperial communications never ceased to be a very awkward strategic problem.

According to Thucydides,[17] fear, self-interest, and glory are the three mainsprings that move mankind, and all three are manifest and larger than life in the history of the two empires. Glory and honour, overlooked and rather forgotten today, were tremendous driving-forces. Cicero says that a thirst for glory steeled the Romans to fight their wars to victory;[18] and to many Victorians and Edwardians the road to Mandalay seemed something more than a mere traffic artery with commercial possibilities, while forbidden Lhasa became the goal of a British expeditionary force largely because it was there. Even today glory still retains its lustre in literature. *La Gloire de l'Empire* has been chosen, in irony or in earnest, by the brilliant French author, Jean d'Ormesson, for the title of his recent *tour de force* on an imaginary state and its rise to greatness.[19] And even the barest accounts of the daring enterprise and exploits of Elizabethan mariners, with their practical genius and their panache, have not lost their power to enthral.

If selfish exploitation with its limited scope had continued to characterize the Roman and the British Empires, they would have been little more than episodes in the human story: they would certainly not have made the impact that they unquestionably did on history. It was when the swashbuckling attitudes and the buccaneering habits of their earlier periods gave way to broader and more responsible approaches that they attained their true greatness. As a result, instead of remaining episodes, they became epochs.

2

'Land of Hope and Glory'

Both Rome and the British Empire, once they reached their
culminating maturity, achieved that rarest phenomenon, a
long interval of peace. The advantages of peace were
immense in both empires, the more impressive when set
against the previous circumstances of the subjected lands
and peoples. It achieved security and prosperous order, and
spread and preserved the highest forms of civilization of the
time. Roman engineering and British technology changed
and improved conditions in the world. But while the
assimilating principles of Roman government led to a unity
hitherto unknown in the ancient world, the British ideal of
imperial trusteeship promoted nationalism and independence in the dependent countries.

The Roman Empire enjoyed its heyday in the first two
centuries A.D., during which period it reconciled its
inhabitants to the idea of Roman rule and achieved a
considerable degree of unity. It owed this success
chiefly to its remarkable absorptive powers.

   The Empire consisted of all sorts and conditions of
men speaking a wide variety of tongues, professing all
kinds of religious beliefs, different from one another in
their ways of life and the cultural levels that they had
attained, the Romans themselves being the ruling
people. But the Romans were not an exclusive sect,
intent on keeping all the lesser breeds beyond the pale.

It was possible for the inferior, subject peoples of the Roman Empire to obtain Roman citizenship and thus themselves become Romans.

From their earliest beginnings the Romans had been quite willing to admit others to their citizenship, and for a very practical reason. As Philip the Fifth, king of Macedon in the third century B.C., noted, the policy enabled them to outnumber their rivals.[20] But it was a generous as well as a practical policy and the Romans adhered to it, almost uninterruptedly, throughout their history.

Admittedly, to acquire Roman citizenship was a privilege, not an obligation, and in the first two centuries A.D. it was usually reserved for those who were prepared to talk, think, and act like Romans. Not that this meant forced, compulsory assimilation. Non-Romans were not obliged to learn Latin, become converts to Rome's religion, or adopt Roman customs. The Roman authorities were gratified if the native provincials did so, but they did not use compulsion. They preferred the carrot to the stick, relying chiefly on the force of attraction and privilege.

After 27 B.C. the maladministration of earlier years decreased markedly. Rome then ceased to be a Republic. She came under the rule of emperors, the first of whom, Augustus, reformed and revitalized her Empire. The evidence of improvement is clear and insistent. For one thing, the Roman provinces now obtained much greater security, and came to enjoy the boundless majesty of the Roman peace, to use the famous expression of the Elder Pliny; and the Elder Pliny ought to have known, for he was himself an official of the Empire, and in more than one province.

Now a province of the Roman Empire was not like a province of Canada. It did not have a legislature or anything resembling our provincial departments. It was, in fact, a geographical expression, not a political entity, but rather a collection of political entities. It was an aggregate of separate states, roughly comparable to our counties in size. Some of them were tribal, others urban. The Romans preferred and favoured the latter sort, the city-states as they have been called; but their Empire always contained many of the former, tribal communities whose degree of development did not warrant their organization as civic commonwealths of the municipal kind.

Thus a Roman province had no centralized administration except in the person of its frequently changed governor. Apart from him the only province-wide institution was a committee of dignitaries who could serve as a sounding-board for provincial complaints, but whose principal function amounted to little more than encouraging the natives to practise the Roman equivalent of standing to attention for the playing of 'God Save the Queen'. For prudential reasons Rome took care to have no provincial organs of administration: a province might be large enough to be dangerous. Instead, she granted self-government at local level, the level of the small states collectively making up the province. It was in them that the everyday tasks of administration were carried out by local councils and local officials chosen from the local inhabitants. These, manifestly, were not sovereign states, since they were not permitted to have a foreign policy of their own. But they were self-governing states; and even though in the last analysis they were controlled by Rome and paid taxes to her, their autonomy was surprisingly extensive. So was their security.

It was the merit of the emperor Augustus to make careful provision for the peace of the provinces. The Roman armed services in the days of the Republic had been curiously makeshift. Field forces had been raised as needed by conscripting Roman citizens, the inducted soldiers remaining on active service for the duration of the need. For this haphazard arrangement the emperor Augustus substituted a permanent standing army in which the men serving were not short-term draftees but career soldiers, who had signed on for a long period, usually for twenty-five years. The Roman imperial army Augustus thus created amounted in all to between 300,000 and 350,000 men in the first two centuries A.D., and, although this is a very large figure by ancient standards, it would be wrong to think that it made the Roman Empire bristle with armaments. On the contrary, except in frontier districts, the army was usually very unobtrusive; and, even in the frontier districts, it was barely large enough to do its job. Partly for political prudence and partly for reasons of economy Augustus had made the imperial army as small as possible: it did not have any central reserve and, for certain stretches of the boundaries, it had to rely on the peace being enforced by neighbouring external tribes, paid to perform this task by the Roman authorities, in somewhat the same way that in the Indian Army the British supplemented the forces of their Empire with hired regiments of Gurkhas from Nepal.

On the whole, the Roman imperial army discharged its task with great efficiency during the first two centuries A.D. Although fighting occurred not infrequently along the frontiers, the peace of the inner provinces was largely undisturbed. Even the rigours of billeting decreased, since permanent camps were built for the troops in many areas.

The Pax Romana thus enforced made the Roman Empire very attractive for those who lived within its borders. It came to be regarded as the region of ordered and civilized living, the *oikumene* to use the Greek word commonly adopted to describe it, a word that has now passed into our own language even if normally with a rather different connotation. The world beyond was the barbarous region where lawlessness and anarchy were rife. Inside the *oikumene* the rule of law prevailed.

It would be absurd, of course, to suggest that the millennium had now arrived and that Augustus' reforms had transformed the misruled world of the Roman Republic into a Utopia of unalloyed happiness. Things had undoubtedly improved, but they had not become perfect. Opportunities for illicit money-making still existed, ranging all the way from simple acceptance of bribes for favours to prostitution of the courts of justice, and worse. The Elder Pliny records having seen Lollia Paullina, who had been briefly married to the emperor Gaius, gleaming with pearls and emeralds. The observant Pliny notes their worth which, translated, would be about four million of today's dollars, and these gorgeous jewels had not been lavished upon her by her prodigal emperor husband, but, as she readily declared, had been inherited from her grandfather, purchased (so Pliny indignantly stressed) with loot from the provinces.[21]

One area offering scope for unscrupulousness was provincial taxation. Rome's action in taxing her provinces at all seems shocking to people nurtured on the doctrine of no taxation without representation. Yet it is difficult to see how there can be administration without taxes.

One aspect of Roman tax-raising, however, seems very unfair. The provinces in effect subsidized Italy, since its inhabitants paid much less. And it was not just the varying levels of the taxes, but also their very existence that was the source of evil. It opened the door to corruption and illegal exactions. Bribery to avoid discrimination or to obtain privilege at the hands of Roman officials was common, and the emperors could not stop it, no matter how conscientious they were, since really close control from Rome was impossible in an age of oar-propelled ships and animal-drawn wagons.

The historian Tacitus describes some of the ingenious but rascally tricks to which the officials resorted; and it was largely the activities of a money-grubbing procurator that provoked the bloody revolt of British tribes under Boudicca in A.D. 60/61.[22] That revolt was mercilessly suppressed, but in fairness one should add that the peccant procurator was immediately removed.

The Romans could claim, of course, that if they were taking taxes out of the provinces, they were also giving something in return: they were providing law, order, and peace. Cicero actually made this claim under the Roman Republic. But it could be put forward with far greater justice from the time of Augustus on and indeed Tacitus does so. The Roman imperial army did then provide security.

The peace was favourable to economic initiative, and enterprising men who knew how to exploit it naturally prospered. Fortunes were not made only by the ruthless exploiters of provincials. For men of enterprise, ability, and industry opportunities to prosper were not lacking; and, even though there were degrees of privilege, there is abundant evidence to show that all classes in the Empire might do well, if luck was on their side. Even for slaves the outlook was not altogether bleak. Inscriptions and literature alike reveal that many of them won their freedom and put it to good use.

Augustus insisted that the most privileged group in the Empire should be the Roman citizens.[23] In the first instance, this meant the inhabitants of Italy. But, by Augustus' day Roman citizens were also to be found in increasing numbers outside of Italy, in other words, in the provinces; and there they were better off than their non-Roman fellows. Their social status was higher; they enjoyed better protection at law; and their opportunities for preferment into positions of prestige and influence were infinitely greater. Nor did the Empire make particularly heavy demands upon them. In the first two centuries A.D. Roman citizens were seldom, if ever, conscripted for service in the armed forces. On the contrary, those of them who wished to do so could pursue the even tenor of their way, and might even pass their entire lives, without their peace and quiet ever being unduly disturbed. This, incidentally, was in marked contrast with the boisterous state of affairs that had prevailed in the Roman Republic during the last century B.C., when the inhabitants of both Italy and the provinces had found civil wars, confiscations, and violence ruinously rampant.

But the well-ordered existence enjoyed by the Roman citizens was within the reach of all, since, as we have noted, all inhabitants of the Empire were eligible for the citizenship. In any province, once one of its small states became thoroughly Roman in language, habits, and outlook, it was likely to be designated as legally 'Roman': that is, it ceased to be 'peregrine' (foreign), its burgessses becoming Roman citizens. Provincial communities were continually acquiring Roman citizenship in this way.

For non-Roman individuals, as distinct from entire communities, there was another and a quicker route to the citizenship, by way of service in the Roman imperial army. Roman citizens could, of course, enlist if they had a mind to, but in fact they seldom did; and as the Empire got older, their reluctance to do so became ever more marked. It almost looks as if exemption from military service came to be regarded as one of the chief privileges of the citizen-born. They were the favoured group: and they complacently assumed that the invincible Empire needed no exertions from them. So the Roman imperial army came to be recruited from those who did not possess the Roman citizenship, that is from the provincials. But, if these men did not possess it when they joined the army, they certainly did when they left it. Some of them, the legionaries, got the Roman citizenship on enlistment; others, the auxiliaries, on their discharge. But one way or another, all who served obtained it. The army was thus a most potent factor in spreading the Roman citizenship. And not merely the citizenship. The army was also instrumental in spreading Roman ways and the Latin language. It was the provincial communities, the small states of the Empire, the local towns and municipalities that provided the backbone of the Roman army, supplying it not only with its other ranks, but also—and increasingly—with its centurions or junior officers. After their years of service these men, now become Roman citizens, settled down, not as a rule in Italy (which few of them knew at all well, since units of the Roman imperial army were not normally stationed in Italy during the first two centuries A.D.), but in the provinces, either in those provinces from which they had originally come or in those where they had done their service. Many of them, especially the ex-centurions, played an active part in the affairs of the provincial communities where they settled;[24] and once ex-soldiers had romanized a community, Roman citizenship would soon be forthcoming for it, even for its stay-at-homes who had never joined the army.

But although Roman citizenship improved men's status, it did not automatically elevate them to influence. The Romans were no believers in equality, and they reserved positions of eminence for the talented and the energetic, preferably among the well-to-do.[25] To that end, the Roman population was carefully stratified.

Below the all-powerful emperor at the summit stood the senatorial aristocrats, wealthy, haughty, and few: in the whole Roman Empire at any one time there were hardly more than seven hundred of them; and, no matter where they originally came from, once they became Roman senators, they tended to congregate in Italy. Below these senators there was a second aristocracy, it too quite wealthy but considerably more numerous. This was the equestrian order, with their numbers running into the thousands, although, being spread over the whole Empire, they could not have seemed particularly common. Together, the two aristocracies provided the Empire with its highest officials, administrators, and senior army officers, certain posts being exclusively reserved for senators, and others no less exclusively for equestrians.

The overwhelming mass of Roman citizens, however, were simply plebeians and had little or no say in the

formulation and direction of policy, or in the appointment of officials, except possibly at the purely local
level: and even there, in the municipal towns and other
small states that made up the Empire, the voice of the
ordinary man in the street did not sound very loudly.
At the municipal, as at the higher, level an oligarchy
was in control.

Thus the Roman Empire, quite obviously, was
hierarchical, with Roman citizens, the preferred group,
themselves divided into categories. But this was no
closed caste system. There was social mobility as well as
social stratification. We have already seen that
'peregrines', that is non-Romans, could, and did,
become Roman citizens, and in ever-increasing numbers; and, within the Roman citizen body, plebeians
who prospered could become members of the equestrian
aristocracy. Equestrians, in their turn, might become
senators. Finally, it was from the ranks of the latter that
emperors were obtained. Nor was a man's ultimate
origin seriously held against him. Even if race prejudice
does occasionally manifest itself in the literature of the
Roman Empire, as for instance in the writings of the
satirist Juvenal, racism was certainly ignored in
practice.

The entire process is illustrated by the evolution of
the senatorial aristocracy. Just before the birth of
Christ the Roman senate consisted almost exclusively
of Italians, a very high proportion of them coming
from the city of Rome itself. Yet by A.D. 68, when the
first dynasty of Roman emperors came to its end with

the death of the notorious Nero, many of the senators were no longer Italians but Roman citizens from the provinces, prevailingly the western provinces, such as Gaul and Spain. Such provincial senators seem to have come at first from Italian families that had emigrated into the overseas provinces, years and in some instances centuries earlier. But soon unadulterated provincials, from families without any Italian background whatsoever, began to find their way into the senate at Rome, and, once started, this trend gathered speed. By A.D. 100 it was not merely the western provinces that were supplying senators, but the eastern ones as well, the ones that normally, and with full Roman encouragement, spoke Greek. By A.D. 200 senators from Italy were no longer in the majority.

The equestrian aristocracy was equally diversified. Its members came from every nook and cranny of the Roman world, some of them being even of servile extraction.

Thus the aristocracies from which the high imperial officials were obtained might be anything in origin. The emperor's body of advisers, for instance, the *consilium principis* as it was called, contained notables from many different regions of the provinces; and these were the men right next to the seat of power.

Governors of provinces, commanders of legions, and various other lofty dignitaries were all likely to be men of provincial extraction. Moreover, the policy of not sending a man to a post in his province of origin, in case he might build up a home power base there, had the effect of thoroughly scrambling the aristocracy. The co-opting of provincial notables undoubtedly deprived the provincial communities of many men of talent, but it also meant that with the passage of time the governing class in the Roman Empire became cosmopolitan to an extent not even remotely attained in the British.

The Roman emperors themselves, being regularly drawn during the first two centuries A.D. from the ranks of the Roman senate, conform to the pattern. By A.D. 100 a man from the western provinces had become emperor: he was from a family, originally Italian, that had emigrated many years earlier to Spain. By A.D. 200 there was an emperor of provincial birth from Africa who seems to have had no Italian blood whatever in his veins. Until then all the emperors of provincial extraction had come from the Latin-speaking west. But soon after A.D. 200 the purple of the Caesars was being worn by someone from the Greek-speaking east, in the person of a Syrian.

And these emperors were cosmopolitan as well as provincial. Antoninus Pius (A.D. 138–61), who had a Gallic background, was married to a woman with a Spanish one. Antoninus' successor, Marcus Aurelius (A.D. 161–80), also had a Spanish background, while his wife's was very mixed: Spanish, Gallic, and Italian. Septimius Severus (A.D. 180–211), the emperor from Africa, had a woman of Carthaginian or Libyan origin for his first wife and of Syrian for his second. But despite their heterogeneous backgrounds these emperors were not generally regarded, and certainly did not regard themselves, as non-Roman. On the contrary, they were much more likely to be positively ultra-Roman in sentiment. Septimius Severus, for instance, who is said to have been more at home in Punic than Latin, gives the impression of being intent on conforming completely to Roman mentality and conduct. It was with his active encouragement that the famed jurists Papinian and Ulpian developed Roman law, Rome's most precious bequest to later ages, into its most mature and classical form. Septimius' outlook was certainly anything but narrowly north African. His aim was to promote the good government and welfare of the Roman Empire as a whole.[26] Nor was Septimius alone in such devotion to Rome. Some little time after him, an Arab became emperor, and the most notable event of his reign was the celebration, with éclat and splendour, of the one thousandth anniversary of Rome's foundation.

Nothing, of course, could illustrate the success of the Roman policy of assimilation so spectacularly as the rise of provincials to the absolute pinnacle of power. It meant more than mere acculturation of indigenous natives. It implies genuine integration; and as Sir Ronald Syme stressed in a former and very notable series of Whidden Lectures, this was a fact of cardinal importance.[27] In the past Romans had gone out from Italy into the provinces; now in due course and in the fullness of time, provincials in their turn were coming to Rome, there to reinforce and renew the governing classes.[28]

It is this remarkable and widespread assimilation of the upper strata that so sharply differentiates the Roman Empire from the British, where unification of this kind did not occur. Like the Romans, Englishmen did go out into the empire. But there was little traffic in the opposite direction, no reverse flow, so to speak. The Roman world, like modern America, was an extraordinary melting pot, and in it the pervasive Roman ingredient was a unifying factor. The common ground for its men and women, the one thing that characterized them, was their adoption of Rome's language, manners, and outlook: they could all become Roman citizens and consider themselves Roman.

It might be argued that successful assimilation of this kind prevailed only in the upper levels of the population and that the situation must have been very different among the common people. As it happens, little is known about the latter, apart perhaps from those living in Rome itself, and they actually are proved by inscriptions on tombstones to have been quite cosmopolitan. The lower classes in the Empire at large are seldom mentioned in Roman literature, and they did not record anything in their own native tongues. Not that the absence of documents in languages other than Latin and Greek means that the native vernaculars had died out in the first two centuries A.D. They certainly continued to be spoken, for they came to the surface again in the fourth century A.D., when the Roman Empire was breaking up and revitalization movements, as the anthropologists call them, got under way.

Probably the lower orders were not as cosmopolitan and commingled as the aristocracies. The poor could not afford to move far from their places of origin and were not likely to meet, and intermarry with, their opposite numbers from other parts of the Empire.

In this connection, however, the effect of the army should not be overlooked. For a considerable part of the first two centuries A.D., the emperors thought it dangerous to have soldiers serve in their countries of origin; and by serving away from their native heaths, the soldiers became much more romanized than they would otherwise have been. Inevitably, too, they formed unions with women from the districts where they served and they must have helped to romanize them to some extent. If the policy of having soldiers serve far from their original homes had been persisted in, romanization would probably have made still more extensive and penetrating headway throughout the Roman world. It might have been as thoroughgoing everywhere as it came to be in the Iberian peninsula and in Gaul, where, despite the survival of Basque in Spain and the continuance of spoken Celtic near Paris and elsewhere until the fourth and even the fifth century A.D.,[29] the triumph of Latin was so overwhelming that it has remained as the official language, in the form of Spanish, Portuguese, and French, right down to the present day.

In any case, one should not attach undue importance to the slowness, or even the failure, of romanization among the lower orders. In any community the group that set the fashion and decided what attitude should be adopted towards the Empire, was the well-to-do minority. They were the leaders of their communities, and on the whole they were pro-Roman.

One might well ask why. The glib reply that in those days the force of nationalism was much less strong than it is today is not the full explanation.[30] It undoubtedly played a much smaller part in the ancient world than in the modern; but its absence does not sufficiently account for the Roman absorptive success.

It is more useful to consider the positive aspects of the Roman Empire. As we have seen, it was regarded as synonymous with the inhabited, civilized world. Those who entered it, whether forcibly or voluntarily, from the outer and more barbarous reaches had come in from the cold, so to speak. What they found was a broad expanse of peace and a fair semblance of order, where rights of property were safeguarded and the well-to-do were bound to be persons of consequence in their own communities and might even enjoy the prospect of still wider horizons. Even those who did not rise high in the Empire's service could not help but be conscious of their membership in a great political organization, where Roman practicality had improved upon Greek instruction to achieve remarkable progress in the art of civilized living. The Roman policy that favoured material betterment, and the Roman peace that made it possible, caused all provincial communities, urban and tribal alike, to remain contented with their lot.

The cities, which it was the conscious aim of Roman policy to develop, were especial showplaces of the Roman achievement, with their chequer-board layouts, their substantial public buildings, their monumental squares, their luxurious bathing establishments, and their amenities of every kind. The striking spectacle they presented was cause for justified civic pride. Life in them was no doubt to a certain extent standardized, but it was a standard at a higher level than the comparatively low level of technology on which it was based might have led one to expect. To this day one cannot gaze without feelings of surprise and wonder at such monuments as the temple of Jupiter at Baalbek in Lebanon, the triumphal arch at Timgad in Algeria, the amphitheatre at Nîmes in France, the theatre at Merida in Spain, the thermal establishment at Bath in England, the palace at Spalato in Yugoslavia, or the remains of the Danube bridge at Turnu Severin in Romania. The engineering achievement is the more impressive when one considers the network of Roman roads that connected the cities and the magnificent aqueducts that converged on them, bringing in their water supply 'as on triumphal arches', as has been finely said.

Over this whole vast area of ordered living, people and goods could, and did, move with great facility and in confident security. True, there were taxes to pay and even some duties on goods in transit; but they seem very mild compared with modern governmental levies. Even though the ordinary man was debarred from political activity and obliged to show respect to his superiors, any man of energy and talent might become one of the superiors. Think of the amazing career of a certain Marcius Agrippa about the year A.D. 200. This person had started life as a slave, but after winning his freedom he made his way into the equestrian aristocracy and later, more surprisingly, into the senatorial: he even became consul at Rome and governor of more than one important province.[31] Marcius Agrippa was clearly quite exceptional. The average man certainly did not have so heady, enterprising, and exhilarating an experience, and probably felt himself confined to the pursuit of the normal, the unexciting, and the routine. But even if life was humdrum and stereotyped, it could also be comfortable. Edward Gibbon summed it all up two hundred years ago in a famous exaggeration: 'If a man were called to fix the period in the history of the world during which the condition of the human race was most happy and prosperous, he would, without hesitation, name that which elapsed from the death of Domitian to the accession of Commodus'[32] (in other words, A.D. 96 to 180).

It was their contemplation of the panorama of empire that attracted and caught men's imaginations and accounts for their ready acceptance of the notion of a Roman Empire. Even its Greek-speaking inhabitants were won over, despite the determined resistance to romanization which conviction of their own cultural superiority prompted them to offer. When Aelius Aristides, a prominent literary figure of the second-century Greek-speaking world, produced a celebrated oration praising Rome in the most fulsome terms, he was not simply an obsequious time-server. For all the extravagance and flattery of his language, he was undoubtedly saying what many of his compatriots felt.[33]

This was the general attitude of the propertied classes throughout the Empire; and the masses were content to follow their lead, or if they did not actively subscribe to the sentiment they were at least content to tolerate the system.

Even the barbarians living beyond the frontiers were aware of the advantages the Empire conferred. Many of them acquiesced readily, and even eagerly, in their own incorporation, and cases are known of some who actually petitioned for it.[34] Once within the Empire's borders they settled down without more ado, even at a time when the borders were unusually disturbed, as in Marcus Aurelius' reign (A.D. 161–80). Even in the third century A.D., when a time of troubles came upon the Empire and insurrectionary, separatist movements broke out, the numerous uprisings were not so much revolts against Roman authority as protest movements reasserting the Roman character of the Empire, which the rebels thought was being undermined. Later, in the fourth and fifth centuries, when the barbarian invaders (Germans mostly), who had ravaged the Empire in the third century A.D., returned to dismember it completely, they regularly disclaimed any intention or desire of destroying it. On the contrary, whenever they managed to seize and occupy parts of the Empire, they promptly recognized the 'Roman' emperor as the legitimate sovereign authority of the very lands they had annexed. Such was their respect for the Roman Empire and for what they believed it to represent.

The magnetic attraction of the British Empire was not as potent, or at any rate not as durable, as that of its Roman paradigm. The Roman Empire, like the dawn goddess's lover Tithonus, went on for centuries. Over seven hundred years elapsed between the annexation of Sicily and the overthrow of the last 'Roman' emperor in the west, named Romulus Augustulus ironically enough, in A.D. 476. The Greek-speaking eastern half, proudly proclaiming itself Roman and offhandedly referring to the Romans proper as Italians, lasted even longer, until that fatal 29th of May in 1453 when the Osmanli Turks burst into Byzantium. And in the minds and memories of men the empire lived longer still. For centuries, medieval and renaissance Europe nursed the notion, and paraded the formality, of a Holy Roman Empire whose demise, it was believed, would bring the coming of the Antichrist. Perhaps not everyone will agree that, when the Holy Roman Empire was officially pronounced dead on the 6th of August in 1806 and found Napoleon at the height of his glory, medieval fears were justified. But no one will deny that the impact made by the Roman Empire can fairly be measured by the hundreds of years that it remained a forlorn ideal and a nostalgic aspiration.

The British Empire was very short-lived and almost

transitory by comparison. The American colonies formed part of it for less than 200 years. India remained in it rather longer: yet Clive's victory at Plassey occurred less than two centuries before 1948. Many of the African colonies needed much less than even a hundred years for their emancipation. Even so, it is probably remarkable that the British Empire should have lasted as long as it did. After the loss of the American colonies in 1776 its prospects must have seemed dim indeed, despite the continuing allegiance of Canada to the British crown. But by one of those curious coincidences of which history can show so many, developments at once conspired to give birth to a second British Empire. These were the consolidation of British power in India, the opening-up of the antipodean lands, and the birth of the industrial revolution.

When James Watt, observing a boiling kettle in his grandmother's kitchen in the 1760s, was inspired to see how Newcomen's crude experiments could be improved into a workable steam engine, modern technology was born. It is true that, for something like 10,000 years before that, man had possessed a technology of sorts. It had been in the year 8000 B.C. or thereabouts that palaeolithic man had stopped being an animal who simply seized and grabbed whatever he needed from nature and became a food producer himself, providing for his own needs. Even so, the primitive technology that he began to develop in those far-off stone age days did not advance very fast or very far. For centuries progress was very slow. From 8000 B.C. to the 1760s A.D. man's output of goods and services *per capita* did not increase to any startling or spectacular extent. Even the Roman Empire, with all its amazing engineering triumphs, had been technologically stagnant. Why it should have been so has been much debated. There is general agreement that it was not because of a too great reliance on slave labour and its lack of incentives. Perhaps, as one of our most distinguished Whidden lecturers suggested, it was due to an ignorance of algebra.[35] Whatever the reason, it was not until the 1760s that technology took the great leap forward that made the industrial revolution possible, and thereafter the pace was rapid. Its effect was to transform the face of the world, and Great Britain was the pioneer and for a long time virtually monopolized the process. She was the workshop of the world, as a popular saying of the last century expressed it.

That this had much to do with the success of the British Empire is obvious. It was industrial strength that enabled Britain with her relatively small population to overcome Napoleon, to become mistress of so far-flung an empire, to maintain control over long and complex sea routes, and to hold her empire with few forces. The peacetime British Army seemed contemptibly small to the German Kaiser; the part of it stationed in India, easily its largest component, numbered considerably fewer than 100,000 men. And to the argument that it was the Royal Navy rather than the Army that was the instrument of power, it can be replied that personnel serving in the fleet were not overwhelmingly numerous either. It was the quality and range of the technology developed by Great Britain that made the Pax Britannica possible.

Some historians go further and argue that her advanced technology kept Britain's empire together and made the overseas territories content to remain a part of it.[36] It provided them with irrigation works, factories, steel plants, and all the myriad products spawned by the industrial revolution; with hospitals, schools, and universities; and above all with the communications (the ports, roads, bridges, railways, telegraphs, and telephones) without which primitive communities had little chance of entering the modern world. For long Britain alone could supply the sinews for the defence of the Empire, and she did so, virtually unaided almost down to the very end of the nineteenth century. The Empire was, quite literally, dependent upon the land of hope and glory.

Things changed, of course, during the nineteenth century. Long before the outbreak of World War I the industrial supremacy of Britain had begun to falter in face of the growing industrial strength of Germany, the United States, and more recently Japan; and by the time of the first world war her technological superiority was clearly a thing of the past. This was to be only too fatally demonstrated in World War II, when the Japanese sank two of the mightiest warships in the Royal Navy with comparative ease and then, immediately afterwards, went on to capture Singapore with forces markedly inferior in numbers to the colony's defenders.

But to recognize the fall of Singapore on that dire 15th of February in 1942 as betokening unmistakably the end of the British Empire, even though Britain and the Commonwealth were ultimately to emerge victorious from the catacylsmic contest of which it was but one incident, does not mean that the Empire began and ended with technology. It was not a structure bolted and rivetted together merely by Sheffield steel.

The smallness of the forces with which it was held and the willingness of its peoples and nations, once they obtained independence from Britain, to remain closely associated with her in the Commonwealth indicate that the imperial tie depended on something more than a certain skill in mechanical, electrical, and civil engineering. Britain's subjects, like Rome's centuries earlier, found the empire, of which they formed a part, by no means totally unacceptable. Indeed some native peoples, the islanders of Fiji, Tonga, and the Gilbert and Ellice group for instance, actually joined the Empire of their own accord, in the same way that alien tribes had sometimes sought admission into the Roman Empire. But the attractiveness did not lie exclusively in the material sphere. Countries like Australia, New Zealand, much of Canada, and parts of Southern Africa felt an attachment to Britain because she had supplied them with the immigrants who settled in them. Clearly, for the Indian sub-continent, for large parts of Africa, and for the islands of the south seas, this could not be the explanation; and it may be doubted whether it was the entire explanation even for the white dominions.

Language had something to do with the matter. English was the mother-tongue for most of the inhabitants of the white dominions. This, once again, was not the case with India and the native colonies. But it is probably true that all of them appreciated the gift of her language from Britain. English as a world tongue enabled them to participate more fully and more easily in international society and to play some role on the world stage; it introduced them to the world of English literature and a much better understanding of English ideals and institutions; and it supplied them with a lingua franca.

But it was not only by bestowing her language any more than by bestowing her technology that Britain reconciled the countries overseas to her imperial role. She won them far more by the methods and, above all, by the spirit and purpose of her rule.

The methods, as it happens, bore some resemblance to those of the Romans. The imperial worthies of England, and especially the men who fashioned the second British Empire, almost without exception had had a classical education, and their study of Latin and Greek had made them very familiar with the Roman Empire as depicted by Tacitus and others. Their interpretation of it, whether fanciful or not, provided inspiration and some instruction, even though theirs

was a very different world and a very different age—
an age familiar with the lessons of 1776, exposed to
French egalitarian doctrines, and imbued with the
spirit of Victorian humanitarianism.

The Romans could teach them something about the
responsibility of governors to the governed and also
something about methods of indirect rule. In fact, like
the Romans, the British availed themselves of the ruling
and administrative elements already existing in the
overseas territories. British Residents, Political and
District Officers and Commissioners and other officials
regularly sought to work through sultans, emirs, tribal
chiefs, and similar native authorities. But the British
faced a situation of infinitely greater complexity than
the Romans ever did. Extreme differences of climate
and environment presented them with races and
cultures that were starkly unlike one another. No
uniform system of dealing with them was possible, and
no precedents existed, not even in the Roman Empire
which was the only previous one to be even remotely
similar to their own. To cope with the bewildering
diversity with which they were faced the British were
forced to improvise. The system that they devised
varied all the way from rudimentary paternalism in the
most primitive areas to responsible government, with
features that Britain herself thought worthy of imitation
in the white dominions. In India some states had
representative government granted by Britain, while
the princely ones resembled the so-called client kingdoms of the Roman Empire: their rulers, maharajahs,

THE NEMESIS OF EMPIRE

rajahs, and princes, recognized Britain as the paramount power. But in many particulars British administrative methods were quite dissimilar from Roman, and the results they produced were naturally also very different. Integration of the Roman kind was conspicuous by its absence.

Of course, the hereditary nature of the British monarchy made it impossible for a Canadian, an Australian, a New Zealander, or even a princely Indian, to ascend the throne at Westminster in the way that Spaniards, Africans, and others had become emperors at Rome. But there was theoretically no reason why truly eminent sons of the overseas empire should not have occupied other lofty posts. Yet they did not do so. The British Prime Minister, and his Cabinet ministers too, regularly came from Great Britain. Admittedly to become prime minister or cabinet members at Westminster men from the overseas empire would have had to stand for election to parliament in the old country, and individuals have occasionally and successfully done so, including a native or two of India. But it is hardly likely that they would ever have got to the highest positions in the land. As long ago as the fourteenth century the English people showed by their rejection of Piers Gaveston how they resent authority being wielded over them by the overseas subjects of their own monarch. The British Prime Minister in the earlier part of this century who was born in Canada of an Ulster background is the exception to prove the rule, and Bonar Law, be it remembered, had not been long out of his cradle when he left Canada for good to settle in Britain.

It should not have been beyond the wit of man to devise a political system that would have harnessed and exploited to advantage the best and most capable talents from all over the Empire. Yet the only overseas members who went to Westminster in their own right were Irishmen, remarkably enough.

Only during the supreme crisis of war was there some change. An imperial war cabinet composed of the dominion prime ministers was improvised in World War I; and in the cabinets that directed the British effort in both the world wars of this century, the overseas countries had some representation, Smuts of South Africa participating in that of World War I and Casey of Australia in that of World War II. But even this small degree of integration ended with the fighting; and the white dominions had their own delegations at the peace conferences and entered the League of Nations after the first, and the United Nations after the second, world war as separate members.

Moreover, dominion abilities were not much used at lower levels of administration than the cabinet. In the main, officials for imperial posts came from schools like Eton and Harrow, or the universities of Oxford and Cambridge.

One result of the exclusion of the dominions was to throw them back upon themselves. Able men channelled their political ambitions into the service of their own communities rather than into the service of the

Empire as a whole; and the countries overseas thus retained virtually exclusive use of the abilities and talents of their own distinguished sons. This brought them incalculable benefit, but it also contributed powerfully to the growth of local nationalisms.

This aspect of British imperial affairs is in striking contrast with the situation in the Roman Empire. It is explained by the entirely different purposes the two empires were seeking to serve. The aim of the Romans was assimilation, that of the British almost exactly the opposite. They came to conceive their task as being the protection and the advancement of the native races. Where the Romans tolerated local languages, cultures, and ways of life, the British promoted them, insisting that the development of the indigenous peoples came first. Undoubtedly there was some hope of economic advantage mixed in with their policy of assisting the less developed countries to political maturity. But, on the whole, their impulse to promote native well-being prevailed; and the spokesman of the British government in 1923, a Conservative government as it happened, was quite sincere in saying: 'His Majesty's Government think it necessary to record their considered opinion that the interests of the African nation must be paramount. . . . His Majesty's Government regard themselves as exercising a trust on behalf of the African population.'[37]

Thus the British were deliberately preparing the native races, first for representative government, and then after that for responsible government. The British

officials in the overseas dependencies themselves tried
to set an example of the kind of administration that
they hoped the native peoples would ultimately
establish. The British Residents, District Officers, and
magistrates conscientiously strove to be objective, fair,
and incorruptible. As one of them recorded: 'We see
ourselves as Trustees who are to hand over their trust
at the earliest practical moment.'[38]

There was perhaps some cant in their moral arro-
gance, and many of them could undoubtedly be
described as smug, stand-offish, and insufferably
superior. They could, however, rarely be described as
dishonest or callously indifferent.

The pace of progress towards full responsible
government varied from one country to another in the
British Empire. A series of reforms had brought India
very close to the status of the white dominions, when
World War II broke out and probably caused some
postponement of the final step. In Africa where
conditions seemed less mature, the transition was
slower.

In the case of both India and Africa, and of the
colonies generally, impatient critics, many of them in
Britain itself, levelled charges of dilatoriness on the part
of officials and of bad faith on the part of the government in Westminster.[39] Others, however, remembering
the laboured birth of responsible government in Canada
and Australia and noting what has been happening
recently in certain regions, wonder whether the
approach towards self-government may not in some

cases have been too swift. In any case, no one will deny that the Empire did represent an amazing experiment in human organization.

But the British attempt to convert native peoples into modern nations ended as the Roman attempt to transform native peoples into Romans had ended, in the loss of empire.

3

'Westward the Course of Empire'

Both the Roman and the British imperial powers disintegrated under the changing conditions within them. In Rome, the constant adoption of new elements from the provinces, which had been an invigorating factor in Roman life, got out of hand and became excessive. The character and the structure of Roman government were gradually flooded with foreign practices and remained Roman only in name before it collapsed. The British imperial government was caught in the ferment of nationalisms which it had encouraged and which precipitated its dissolution.

The disintegration of the Roman Empire has been a theme for discussion and speculation for the past fifteen hundred years, in fact ever since the days of Saint Augustine.

The usual explanation, that it perished because it was laid in ruins by repeated attacks of invading 'barbarians', Germans for the most part, while no doubt true, appears much too superficial and limited. It does not reveal why primitive and disunited barbarians, and not particularly numerous barbarians either, were able to wreak their will and make a mockery of the boundless majesty of the Roman peace. No single cause can give a complete answer. An overriding explanation must go deeper. I suggest that it is to be found in the way that the Empire was gradually transmuted into something new and strange, so that as a *Roman* empire it simply ceased to be. An increasing and ultimately an overwhelming flood of men, attracted by the prestige of Rome but of outlook different from hers, infiltrated into the centre of power. The quality, system, and principle of Roman government were diluted in this foreign stream, and the governing class, no longer based on Roman traditions and purposes, became in fact un-Roman.[40]

Originally, Romans were to be found only in Rome and its immediate environs, in the part of Italy known as Latium. They were a group of farmer-soldiers, devoted to their own community and dedicated to its survival. That survival, they were convinced, depended upon a right relation with its gods and upon their own willingness to submit to the authority deriving from high birth, valour, and service to Rome; and out of this conviction they were ready to defer to the policies of their leaders and to follow them with obedience, discipline, and tenacity. Within their own community they were guided by a legalistic instinct for what was customary; outside it, they were prompt to defend it, and to assert it. And the name Rome summed up their community: their aspirations, laws, hopes, and ambitions all centred on Rome.

By the last century B.C. they had expanded from Latium all over the Italian peninsula, and where they had not installed themselves as settlers they had annexed and incorporated. But they accomplished this

spread over Italy without becoming themselves radic-
ally changed. No matter how different in language,
outlook and general culture the other peoples of Italy
originally were from the Romans (and some of them
were very different), close and enduring contact had
made it possible for all of them over the centuries to
coalesce without basically altering the character of the
Romans themselves. No doubt developments, the
passage of the years, and the admixture of Italian
elements made the Romans of the first century B.C.
somewhat different in character from those of the sixth
and fifth. Even so, a real fusion of Romans and Italians
had taken place. It had largely meant the conversion
of the Italians to Roman viewpoints, habits of thought,
and patterns of life. The two could not be easily
distinguished from one another, and in fact the Greek-
speaking inhabitants of the eastern end of the Mediterranean did not make any distinction between them. By
the beginning of the Christian era the unification was
complete, and henceforth all Italians could fairly be
reckoned Romans.

Unification of provincials with Romans, however,
did not prove similarly possible. The Romans did have
a remarkable talent for assimilating others; but the
tribes and peoples of their Empire were too multifarious,
the distances, both physical and spiritual, separating
them from Italy were too great, and the number of
Italians settled in their midst too small to make their
total romanization possible. Accordingly the fusion of
old Romans and new, of Italians and provincials, of

westerners and easterners, and of all the assorted types within the Empire was never fully accomplished. The ripples caused by a stone thrown into a pond get smaller and feebler the further they are from the point of impact. So it was in the Roman Empire, despite repeated and frequent extensions of the Roman citizenship, which reached their climax *c.* A.D. 212 when the emperor Caracalla decreed that all freeborn inhabitants of the Empire, with very few exceptions, were henceforth to be Roman citizens, in other words officially Romans.

At the time of Caracalla's decree much of the Roman Empire must have been still unassimilated. The diverse peoples and races that composed it had not been completely made over; and variations in the duration of their submission meant differing degrees in the extent of their acculturation. Even in the most thoroughly romanized provinces, those of the Iberian peninsula and Gaul, many of the lower classes could have been only superficially affected, if that, to judge from the survival of the local vernaculars into the Late Empire.

A high degree of romanization had indeed taken place among the upper classes all over the Empire. But even in their case it was never absolute, no matter how self-consciously Roman a provincial notable might try to become. Provincials might, and indeed they often did, become fervent Roman patriots: one thinks of Julius Classicianus from Gaul, the servant of the Empire in Britain; of Licinius Sura from Spain, the

intimate of the emperor Trajan; of Plutarch, the
engaging writer of biographies, and of Herodes Atticus,
the noted philanthropist, both of them from Greece.
Yet they must always have been Romans with a
difference. Their way of looking at things, even if they
were not always aware of it, would not be exactly the
same as the Romans' way; and the vestigial remains of
their alien background assumed importance as, in the
course of time, age-old Roman institutions and customs
changed. The Roman senate itself was greatly altered
as the result of the steady infiltration of provincials into
its ranks.

Transmutations of national character and culture are
by no means easy to trace. Change of language, even
when it can be clearly documented and measured, is
not in itself conclusive, as English-speaking Irishmen
abundantly prove. What really matters is intellectual,
emotional and spiritual re-orientation, and this is not
easily quantifiable. It can be revealed, however, by
men's customs and practices.

One age-old Roman habit, to which Cicero under
the Republic and Tacitus under the Early Empire call
attention,[41] was that of having high state officials serve
indifferently in either civilian or military posts. One
year a man might be an important administrator; in
the next he might serve as a general. Normally the
Roman emperors continued this republican practice,
since they were not eager to create specialists who might
too easily be mistaken for symbols of state authority.[42]
Nevertheless, in the first two centuries A.D. a tendency

to depart from the venerable practice gradually developed. Functionaries began to be reassigned to the same areas or to similar tasks, once they had acquired experience and demonstrated competence in them. An army officer who did well in a certain province was likely to find himself posted to it time and again: Agricola, for instance, was ordered to Britain repeatedly during the first century A.D. A civilian, who possessed a certain type of expertise, was likely to be called upon to exercise it on more than one occasion: the Younger Pliny, for instance, served on several financial boards about the beginning of the second century A.D. As time went on, specialization of this kind led, logically and inexorably, to the separation of civilian and military functions; and, from the middle of the second century A.D. on, it proved possible for a man to have an all-military career, without serving much, if at all, in civilian posts.

The consequences of this may have been unforeseen, but they were certainly far-reaching. Whereas previously a serving soldier could hardly rise above the rank of centurion, from the late second century A.D. on he could advance into the highest officer class; and from there it was but a short step to the imperial purple.

This was soon revealed. In A.D. 235 a Thracian peasant, who had passed his entire adult life in military camps, was acclaimed by his troops as emperor of the Romans. Thus, a man practically without any experience of civilian life had come to occupy the most powerful position in the Roman, and indeed in the then known world.[43] Ominous as this development was, it became even more so a quarter of a century later when senatorials were completely debarred from serving as officers. For the quality of the troops was by then becoming increasingly dubious.

By the third century A.D. military disorder had made a vastly increased army necessary. According to Lactantius, a contemporary, the army had grown by A.D. 300 to a size four times as large as it had been under the emperor Augustus at the time of Christ. This would mean a standing army of a million men or more, a staggering and impossible figure. Lactantius must be exaggerating. Nevertheless, it is quite certain that by his day the army had been greatly enlarged. The emperor Septimius Severus had found it necessary to increase it with a central reserve about A.D. 200; and just over half a century later the emperor Gallienus strengthened the army still further by adding a large cavalry striking force to it.

The enlargement of the army did more than just revive the horrors of billeting. It created a most awkward problem, since it came at the precise moment when recruits of average good quality were proving difficult to find. From A.D. 212 on, when all inhabitants of the Empire had been declared Roman citizens, the law of diminishing returns applied. Those born with the Roman citizenship had rarely volunteered for the standing army of the Roman Empire. Provincials, however, had been willing to do so since by serving in the army they obtained the citizenship. But now in

A.D. 212 this principal inducement for them to join up was abolished at a single stroke. Consequently the army had to get its soldiers, more and more, from the wildest and most primitive districts, if not from outside the Empire altogether. It even found itself obliged to accept recruits who, in an earlier age, would have been rejected for failing to meet its physical standards. Under these circumstances, it would not be long before the army would no longer deserve to be called Roman: it would be largely barbarized. Yet this was the force to which was entrusted the defence of the Roman Empire against external attack and the defence of Roman values and traditions. One may well suspect that the military disorder that made the larger army necessary was due, at least in part, to the quality of its recruits.

The vicious circle was thus complete; and the gravity of the situation was all the greater owing to the tendency for officers to come up through the ranks, often without any other qualification than rude fighting ability. The centurions, the real professionals of the Roman imperial army, instead of being reasonably good types from developed and romanized provincial communities, were now likely to be of the same stamp as the men they led: rough, uncouth, and brutal. It is quite literally true that, from the third century A.D. on, such men were only too likely to make their way into the highest positions in the Empire, even, as we have seen, into the office of emperor itself.

Developments in the civilian sphere were also disturbing. The provincials, who won their way to the loftiest administrative positions and helped thereby to give the Roman Empire its cosmopolitan flavour, were naturally the most thoroughly romanized of their kind. But, as Plutarch protests,[44] their appointment to important imperial posts meant serious loss for their own communities, whose romanization slackened and whose administration deteriorated. The quality of local administration would presumably have declined in any event in the euphoric atmosphere of the Roman peace and the carelessness that it engendered. But the brain drain to Rome inevitably aggravated the decline.

Already by the beginning of the second century A.D. the affairs of some communities were so chaotic that they were on the brink of bankruptcy. The reaction of the emperors, at that time men of enlightened responsibility, was to send out high-ranking commissioners of their own careful choosing to the affected areas to put matters to rights. These *correctores*, as they were called, assumed charge over entire regions and the communities within them. True, they were only temporary appointments, but as usual the temporary became the normal and the *correctores* soon developed into a permanent institution. And, of course, they deprived the local officials of their functions. The inevitable effect was substantially to expand the embryonic bureaucracy of Augustus' day. It now began to grow with accelerating speed. By the late third and the fourth centuries A.D. it had burgeoned into the corrupt and greedy monster graphically depicted in the contemporary lament that there were more tax-collectors than taxpayers.

This brought genuine local self-government to an end, and local self-government had been one of the most vitalizing forces in the Roman Empire. Deprived of local outlets for their energies and ambitions, the leading men still remaining in the provincial communities lapsed into indifference and apathy. This in itself was serious enough. But there was also another effect, which does not seem to have been generally appreciated.

As we have seen, the Roman Empire promoted urbanization, since the Romans accepted wholeheartedly the Greek idea that only in the context of the city-state could true civilization flourish. In many parts of her Empire, therefore, Rome had converted tribal communities into urban commonwealths. For unurbanized rustics such a transformation is always uncommonly difficult. We ourselves have witnessed of recent years the sometimes violent dislocations that result when country dwellers are converted too rapidly into city dwellers. In the Roman Empire their readjustment was reasonably smooth so long as they were being shepherded into their new condition by their own traditional and familiar leaders. But after the second century A.D. they were liable to find the local men, whom they had always been wont to follow, replaced by newcomer *correctores* appointed by the distant emperor; and, if this disruptive distortion of the traditional patterns of their tribal society did not make them resentful, it certainly left them rudderless and bewildered. The effect of the separation of the natives from their habitual local leaders was truly disastrous. It meant a withering away at the grass roots and must have been in large part responsible for the Empire's obvious loss of dynamism.

Religious vitality suffered no less than civic. In an earlier age their religious beliefs and practices had promoted the discipline, the cohesion, and the greatness of the Roman people. Their native religion guaranteed the traditional ordering of their society, and it did much else besides. Polybius, that very acute observer from Greece, writing in the second century B.C., attributed the Romans' rise to supremacy precisely to their religion which was instrumental in keeping them strong and united; and Cicero and Horace, writing a hundred years or so after Polybius, subscribe to his opinion.

Now the native religion of the Romans was by definition a bond with the gods, to whom dutiful respect was paid through acts of public ritual to ensure their favour for the Roman state.[45] To discover the will and intentions of the supernatural powers it had been the habit of the Romans, from time immemorial, to resort to a cult practice described as 'taking the auspices': in other words, they looked for omens. If they found unfavourable omens, it meant that the divinities were angry; whereupon they sought to regain divine goodwill by carrying out prescribed acts of ritual with the most painstaking and scrupulous care.

Meticulous observance of the necessary rites went on

unchanged, at the official level, for centuries. In private and at unofficial level, it is true, any kind of weird or outlandish belief and practice was tolerated, provided that it did not promote crime, foster immorality, or provoke public disorder. But the due and proper performance of the rituals demanded by the native Roman religion always remained part of the duties of the servants of the Roman state.

At a place called Dura on the River Euphrates, in eastern Syria, excavation has revealed the quarters of a unit of the Roman imperial army of the third century A.D., by which time, as we have just seen, the soldiers were being obtained from the most remote and backward districts of the Empire. Yet inscriptions found on the site prove that these rough types of the third century A.D. regularly and officially carried out in the Syrian desert the acts of ritual that had been prescribed, centuries earlier, for cultivating the good graces of the deities of agricultural Italy;[46] and they were doing this in a period and in a place where the mystic religions, and even sophisticated faiths such as Christianity and Judaism, had made considerable headway. Dura actually displays the earliest surviving Christian chapel and one of the earliest surviving synagogues.

It is difficult to believe, however, that when Roman soldiers of non-Roman birth and rude upbringing carried out acts of Roman ritual in this way, they really appreciated the significance of what they were doing or could themselves have attached deep importance to it. They were content to assimilate their own indigenous native divinities to appropriate Roman ones and thereby reconcile their own cults with those of Rome. But that is far from saying that they really understood the rites they were celebrating. And what is not understood will end up, sooner or later, by being simply discarded.

Of even greater import was the change that had come over the religious attitude of the upper classes. Now that the governing personnel were recruited from anywhere in the Empire, they inevitably included devotees of the occult and of the grosser forms of magic. This made them very different from the Roman leaders of earlier days who, despite all the trust that (like all the ancients) they reposed in omens and portents, had scorned the cruder forms of superstition. No matter how much the lower class plebeians in Rome believed in voodoo, magical incantations, werewolves, human-headed snakes and the like, the governing élite of the early days had disdained such absurdities. Now, centuries later, the leaders were hardly any more enlightened than the mob. They still meticulously observed the old rituals, but in a very different spirit. Dio, writing in the early third century A.D., conveys the impression that by then the leaders of society and culture were just as superstition-riddled as the masses; and a state whose spiritual pilots and best educated people have rejected rationality has already lost its values and forgotten what it really stands for.[47]

The history of the auspices which enabled the Romans to keep in well with heaven is instructive in this regard. The ancient belief of the Romans, a belief going back to the earliest beginnings of their city, was that the true and only proper custodians of the auspices were a small group of exclusive and hereditary aristocrats known as the patricians.[48] In the absence of a regular priestly caste, which was something that the Romans lacked, it was this handful of aristocrats who were regarded as the ones possessing the right to deal with the gods on behalf of the Roman people. The patricians, of course, normally delegated this right to the head of the state by conferring the auspices upon him. But whenever the headship of the state fell vacant, the auspices 'returned to the patricians' (as the Roman saying expressed it). These, however, began to die out, and to prevent their total disappearance the emperor Augustus created new ones. Thereby he completely changed the character of the patriciate, since it had hitherto been a strictly hereditary aristocracy. The auspices nevertheless seem to have remained under its control, and this, I suggest, explains why in the days of the Roman Empire a new emperor always felt it necessary to seek official recognition in person from the senate in Rome. For it was only there, in the senate, that he would find the patricians who alone could confer the auspices upon him.

By the third century A.D., however, Roman emperors, like the Roman governor Gallio in the New Testament, knew none of these things. As often as not, they were men of non-Roman extraction, men like Maximin the Thracian, Philip the Arab, Decius the Pannonian, and

Diocletian the Illyrian, who had made their way up from the ranks. Ultimately the practice whose *raison d'être* was not really understood was simply allowed to lapse into desuetude. By the middle of the third century A.D. the emperors ceased creating new patricians and by its end they ceased to seek official recognition, and the auspices, from the patricians in the Roman senate.[49]

By A.D. 300 the Roman people no longer enjoyed its old relationship with the gods, while gross forms of superstition and preposterous magic remained.

The emperors themselves did not entirely escape the prevailing patterns of thought. Constantine the Great (A.D. 312–37), for instance, allowed certain beneficial types of the magical arts to be legally practised. During his struggle for empire he had witnessed the halo phenomenon, as it is called, in the heavens: it had taken the form of a cross on the face of the sun. At that time not yet a Christian, he regarded what he had seen, not so much as a mystical revelation, but rather as a victory omen; and, to ensure the protection of the powerful and to him unfamiliar god of the Christians, he sent his soldiers into the crucial battle of the Mulvian Bridge with an emblem painted on their shields that could be interpreted as Christian. The battle resulted in shattering defeat for his rival for the purple, Maxentius, a devotee of magic, be it noted; and Constantine proceeded at once to recognize Christianity as an official religion of the Roman Empire.[50]

As might have been expected, it is in art that the

change from earlier Roman standards is clearly apparent. The most important among the pervading influences were those from the Greek-speaking Near East. These currents spread over the cities of the Mediterranean and into Rome itself. A certain naturalism that had always been present in Roman sculpture and recurrent in Roman painting, the sense of space in the reliefs and frescoes, the descriptive composition, all these Roman features became largely superseded by new concepts and styles, in which the rigidity of the static compositions and the schematic patterns were already anticipating the unreal surfaces and the rhythms of Byzantine art. A most striking change is seen in the imperial portraits. In those of the first two centuries A.D., whether lifelike or idealized, the human and individual quality is stressed. But by the close of the third century the group portrait of the tetrarchs in Venice is a geometric scheme, devoid of any individual humanism. Under Constantine and later the oriental conception of imperial majesty has full sway, in the colossal statues at Rome and Barletta with their rigid formality of style and inscrutable gazes.

Caracalla's enfranchising act exactly one hundred years before Constantine's victory had thus had the most far-reaching repercussions on all aspects of Roman imperial life—the army, administration, religion, art, everything. Above all, the lower classes everywhere had been made Romans overnight. But these lower classes were quite unlike the plebeians of the pre-Christian Roman Republic, even though for reasons of historical continuity the emperors had professed to regard the heterogeneous mob in the city of Rome itself as genuinely descended from the settlers of Romulus, pampering and indulging it.

In A.D. 212 itself Caracalla's action passed without much comment, either because by then the Roman citizenship was no longer much esteemed, or because by then so large a proportion of the provincials already had it that for the remainder to get it was hardly thought worthy of much notice. Even so, the all-embracing act was of the utmost consequence. Its effect was to make the Roman citizen body anaerobic, to use a word that the ecologists have recently brought into vogue. That is, the amount of extraneous material injected into it overtaxed its powers of absorption and, like parts of Lake Erie and the Baltic Sea, it lost its innate capacity for self-regeneration. The original Roman element was simply swamped.

The great mass of Roman citizens were now Roman only in name. The Roman citizenship no longer inspired vigour and responsibility in those who possessed it. Already at the beginning of the second century A.D. Tacitus was hinting that the citizenship had come to mean very little, and this may help to explain why those of citizen birth in the Roman Empire, unlike the sturdy Romans who repelled Hannibal in the third century B.C., were so reluctant to become soldiers. Officially they formed part of the nation that ruled the world, and they evidently felt that this entitled them to sit back and enjoy the benefits of Rome's supremacy.

Surely there was not much point in their becoming members of the ruling race, if it meant that they had to be also a nation of soldiers. The soldier's dangerous trade should be left to the subject peoples.

In earlier days Rome's fortunes, according to Ennius the father of Roman poetry, stood firm on her ancient customs and on the stalwart qualities of her men. But by the third century A.D. the visions of glory, which earlier Romans had had, were no longer a stirring sight. Pride and *élan* belonged to the past and a nation, that had once cherished the Roman citizenship, now in the days of its depreciation sank into listlessness. Dynamic drive had disappeared from the Empire, and with it much else besides.

Crisis was not long in coming. After A.D. 235 and the assumption of the imperial purple by a rude product of the barracks, there was a half century of incredible chaos and confusion. Civil war raged all over the Empire, as commander after commander strove to make himself supreme. Some succeeded, some failed, and some set up separatist regimes. They were all alike in being short-lived. In the fifty years between A.D. 235 and 285 the number of emperors to receive official recognition from the Roman senate was at least fifteen, and the number of pretenders that arose to dispute the title with them infinitely more: it quite literally defies counting. Naturally, as the assorted rivals for the power of the Caesars were fighting one another, the barbarians seized their chance and attacked across the frontiers, looting and spoiling and spreading alarm and despondency on the grand scale. Superimposed upon this military nightmare came social and economic ruin of truly monumental proportions: disease, famine, shortages, inflation, brigandage, piracy, crime, and downright savagery. Trade by barter became common, and ordinary organized living had, to all intents and purposes, broken down.

It is really extraordinary that the Roman Empire did not perish utterly amid the stress, disorder, and violence of this appalling half century. But somehow some sort of restoration was effected, at least in name. But the price was high: nothing less than massive transformation. The Roman Empire emerged from its ordeal entirely changed.[51]

Yet it must be emphasized that it had not been brought to this sorry pass because men had been deliberately disloyal to it or had simply rejected it. On the contrary, not even the most contumacious elements in the Empire would have claimed that they were bent on destroying it or on promoting revolution. By the third century A.D. all parts of the Empire were, in their own somewhat self-conscious estimation, Roman. This was true even of the Greek-speaking areas. Dexippus, a Greek historian and soldier, is an example: he was the patriotic supporter of the Empire who stoutly defended Athens against the Goths in A.D. 268.

By then men may not have fully understood the cult of Vesta, the goddess on whom depended the safety of Rome, but they worshipped her with an outward

devotion to match that of the earliest Romans.[52] In
fact, as the Empire faded, the more desperate became
the efforts to revive the old religion. It was precisely in
the third century A.D. that the note of revival was most
insistently sounded.

The ephemeral 'barrack emperors', as they have
been called, of that tristful third century regarded
themselves not merely as Roman, but as very particularly Roman. They stoutly protested their devotion to
Roman traditions, and they faced the barbarian assail-
ants of the Empire with the resolute courage of
true patriotism. The pretenders also claimed to
be thoroughly Roman. A challenger of the reigning
emperor normally justified his revolt by damning
the ruler as un-Roman: he, the pretender, would
get the Empire back on to a sound Roman path.
Even the rebels, who broke away from Rome in the
third century A.D. to set up a kingdom of their own
in Gaul, claimed that theirs was the true Roman
society, the authentic Roman state, rather than the
debased and corrupt thing from which they had
shaken loose.

Late in the century emperors appeared who succeeded in restoring some kind of order. They were men
from the Danubian region who, subjected more than
others to barbarian assaults, were galvanized into
making fierce resistance and they prolonged in some
fashion the life of the Empire. They themselves regularly laid claim to the title of 'Restorer of the Roman
Empire'. But, like the lady in Hamlet, they were

protesting too much. What they restored was no longer a Roman empire.

Undoubtedly emperors styling themselves Roman continued to reign until late in the fifth century, and in the east for even longer. Indeed they established gorgeous and ceremonious courts where their subjects, also styled Romans, prostrated themselves before the person of the sacred emperors. True Romans would have stared, wide-eyed, in scorn and disbelief, for, as Tacitus records,[53] they prized only the essentials of sovereignty and ignored its vanities. But by that time there was little left that was really Roman. By the fourth century Rome herself had ceased to be the capital or centre of the empire, or even the focal point of its loyalties, despite the continuing magnetism of the name of Rome. The only practical, significant loyalties that there were were of the narrow and parochial kind that made one's own immediate neighbourhood the only thing worth defending. Despite the use of some ancient names and titles, the armed forces and the administrative arrangements had been changed beyond recognition. It was a world of dwindling towns but bloated cities, of crushing taxation and a widening gulf between rich and poor. The few landowners were opulent, the mass of peasants reduced to serfdom. Not only a new art and a new religion, but even a new Latin had emerged. Above all, the geographical unity of the Empire had been destroyed. The once great Roman Empire after 285 was usually, and after 395 permanently, divided into two or more parts, each under a separate monarch and all liable to be whittled away. The idea of a united empire endured, but the reality was sadly different.

It was not, however, treason or disloyalty that had fatally weakened the Empire. A more potent factor had been the growing carelessness with which the citizenship was extended. The once invigorating and generous policy of admitting new elements from the provinces into the ranks of the Romans got out of hand and brought about a transformation of the citizen body. The imprudent prodigality with which the citizenship was bestowed proved to be the nemesis of empire.

It may well be asked what is the bearing of all this on Britain and her dependencies overseas. The British Empire was not the prey of fifty years of military anarchy over the question of who should rule. The Wars of the Roses belonged to a much earlier period of English history. The dissolution of the British Empire, in fact, was preceded, not by half a century of struggle for the throne, but by half a century and more of a single, glorious reign.

Nevertheless, the story of Rome is by no means irrelevant. The British Empire, too, did not disintegrate because of the uncompromising hostility or active ill-will, much less the treason, of its members; and Britain did not lose her empire through disloyalty any more than Rome did. Even when the parting of the ways came, the Union Jack was not shot down by gunfire. It was struck amid ceremonies of mutual goodwill and understanding, with practically every country, as it became independent, electing to remain closely associated with Britain in the Commonwealth. Burma was the exception to prove the rule, and it probably chose to sever the tie completely because the memory of its wartime experience was still so vivid. The British had been unable to safeguard Burma against the Japanese fury in 1942, and, as Machiavelli remarked centuries ago, a prince who cannot defend his subjects will soon find himself without any.

The disintegration of the British Empire came about with the inevitability of logic. After 1800 especially, the imperial power declared publicly and repeatedly that its first consideration was the interest and the welfare of those whom it governed. A statement made by Lord Macaulay in 1833 when he was secretary of the Board of Control for India has become famous: 'We are free, we are civilized, to little purpose, if we grudge to any portion of the human race an equal measure of freedom and civilization.' The overseas dependencies were therefore encouraged to study their own histories, preserve their own identities and develop their own institutions, and they did so in the atmosphere of enthusiastic nationalism that the French Revolution, more than any other single agency, had done so much to unloose. Any hope there may have been, that the various countries, as they reached full political maturity, would be content to remain members of an empire, evaporated in the heat of strong national feelings. When the white dominions themselves set the example of preferring full independence to self-government within the empire, it was impossible for countries that had no ethnic link of any kind with Britain, like India, the African territories, and the island colonies, not to follow suit.

In the white dominions the sense of kinship was not nursed and preserved by any policy of integration such as Rome had practised; and in its absence their inhabitants did not go on feeling like Englishmen indefinitely. The children of emigrants from the Old Country had no memories of their own of Britain and could not identify themselves completely with the attitudes and sentiments of their parents. For that matter, emigrants and exiles are hardly likely to be the most effective transmitters of national feeling. In the Empire countries other than the white dominions there was of course no sentimental barrier at all opposing the positive encouragement to particularism forthcoming from Britain herself. In all Empire countries, therefore, nationalism had full scope.

The oft-made assertion that similar nationalism was unknown in antiquity is not entirely true. The war of the Batavians against Rome in A.D. 69 and 70, to cite but one example, undoubtedly had nationalist overtones.[54] Nevertheless it certainly is true that nationalist feelings did not affect men's outlook, allegiance and behaviour then in the same way that they do now. It is difficult to see how they could have done so in a world of city-states. In, say, the Roman province of Narbonensis, a man never thought of himself as a Narbonensian, but rather as a burgess of Massilia, or of

Forum Julii, or of some other city; and devotion to one's backyard is not the same thing as national feeling.

In the British Empire it was a man's country that engaged his fierce loyalty; and his twentieth-century tendency to make the land where he resided his first concern was reinforced by the self-government that the British had been so liberally willing to grant. The various countries of the Empire were more preoccupied about the success of their own individual societies than about the success of the Empire as a whole. This, in fact, was just as true of Britain as of the others. And it is, of course, something that is entirely natural. For someone who is born and passes his whole life in Canada, the St. Lawrence is bound to have more meaning than the Thames, the more so since the St. Lawrence does not flow into the Thames as the Orontes did into the Tiber.

It has been said that the break-up of the British Empire could have been postponed and perhaps even entirely averted, had the British been willing to grant trade preferences as well as self-government to the overseas countries.[55] Now it is, of course, certain that if the Empire was to be held together, some sort of unifying force was needed. Whether increased imperial trade was the best link was subject to argument, and it was not the only suggestion made to that end. Just after the middle of the nineteenth century (in 1852) a movement advocating full imperial federation was started in New Zealand, but it never made much headway, despite Lord Milner's later revival of the idea (in 1901).[56] In view, however, of the widely held conviction in Britain that trade was the only real purpose of empire, the proposal to set up a system of imperial preferences seemed much more promising. The Australian colonies and Canada were granting tariff concessions to British goods before 1900, and in 1877 South Africa's Cape Colony had advocated a scheme of imperial preferences. In Britain Joseph Chamberlain vigorously supported the notion in 1903, and at the imperial conference in London, four years later, all the overseas statesmen pushed the idea. But it was all to no purpose. Ideas had changed greatly in Britain since the days of James I in the seventeenth century, when tobacco-growing had been forbidden in the British Isles in order to promote prosperity in the American colonies, or since the eighteenth century, when mercantilism had dominated British policy. By the nineteenth century the free-trade doctrines associated with the names of Adam Smith, Richard Cobden, and the city of Manchester held sway. The Corn Laws were repealed in 1846 and Oliver Cromwell's centuries-old Navigation Act a few years later; and the utilitarian determinists were soon proclaiming that, so far as trade was concerned, the Empire was irrelevant.[57] No matter how ardently Canada, or Australia, or the other overseas countries thought that mutual preferential tariffs by increasing the trade would also strengthen the ties between Empire countries, nothing of the kind really materialized. Late Victorian and Edwardian Britain adhered to its free trade and the colonies, as the

dominions were then called, persisted with protection-
ism, even erecting tariffs against Britain herself.

It was not until 1933, and even then in most gingerly
fashion, that the Ottawa agreements introduced
imperial preferences over a fairly wide range of products. And by then it was too late. The Balfour Report
and the Statute of Westminster had been proclaimed
some years previously and W. E. Forster's prediction of
1875 had come true: dependence had been replaced by
association. What was once an empire had become a
commonwealth.

It may well be doubted, however, whether tinkering
with customs duties would really have made much
difference. Trade pacts have never yet proved stronger
than nationalism. It was not the refusal to practise a
kind of closed-shop imperialism, any more than it was
active disloyalty, that ended the British Empire. It was
the paradoxical nature of the Empire itself. In it visions
of imperial greatness faded before strong regional
attachments. The clarion call of the Declaration of
Arbroath, exalting liberty and independence above
glory, had been heard far beyond the borders of
Scotland. The various parts of the Empire were
concerned to stress their own distinctive aspects and
their own interests first and foremost. Immediately
after World War II when Britain was intent on promoting her own welfare society, while Australia and
New Zealand were chiefly concerned about the security
of the Pacific, it was hardly surprising that the two
last-named countries should sign the Anzus pact with

the U.S.A. and that the mother country should remain outside it.

The ruling power's conviction that it owed responsibility to the ruled and that imperial territories were trusts wherein native interests were the overriding consideration, led to the dissolution of the British Empire; and this is in marked contrast with the Roman Empire where such divergent development of its different parts would not have been tolerated. In the Roman Empire disintegration came for a very different reason. Yet in one respect the British break-up does resemble the Roman. In its case, too, the most praiseworthy feature was the one that hastened the end. Nemesis overtook the Empire because liberalism could not be reconciled with imperial rule.

The experiment of empire, whether British or Roman, indicates that the human race is capable of forming large combinations. But it also proves that the human race is no less prone to practise minute fragmentation. Or is atomization a more appropriate word, in view of the recent creation of such minuscule sovereign states as Singapore, Mauritius, and divided Cyprus? One is reminded forcibly of a Roman poet's vision of atoms in the void, fortuitously colliding and coalescing into ever larger organisms, but at other times no less fortuitously splitting up again and going their separate ways. We, however, can hardly share the complacency of Lucretius at the contemplation of such an endlessly repeated cycle of apparently purposeless coalitions and equally purposeless disintegrations. For the formation and dissolution of empires, affecting the lives of myriads of men, are matters of too much consequence. They seem to illustrate man's instinctive lust for power. But in both the Roman and the British Empire much more was involved than the mere lust for power.

The ordered government of the Roman Empire and the civilized security of its romanized cities, the ideal of administrative probity in the British Empire and the political education of its peoples are impressive achievements. For a space each of these two great empires enabled large areas of the world to go about their business in an atmosphere of peace and some prosperity, and they imbued their inhabitants with the feeling that they were participating in a great adventure of human history. And when the adventure ended, bewilderment ensued.

To the Roman Empire there succeeded a welter of contending and competing states and the myriad confusions epitomized in the expression 'the dark ages'. The British Empire has not, it is true, been followed by a breakdown in civilization, at least not as yet. But it has left behind it a power vacuum in which disruption is very much in evidence. Harold Macmillan's 'wind of change' seems not only to have blown away the Empire, but also to have blown in a large measure of discontent, disquiet, and foreboding.

Yet from the ruins of the Roman Empire there finally emerged the vigorous, quarrelsome, but above all brilliant states of Christian Europe; and who can say what may not emerge from the seemingly formless Commonwealth? The sun has indeed set upon the British Empire, but as a Greek poet long ago remarked: 'Even in its setting the sun is ever the same.' It may very well be that the British championing of the liberal temper will lead the world to Sir Winston Churchill's 'broad sunlit uplands'.

Man's attempt to reconcile order and liberty is an old and never-ending chapter in his history; and the creation and decay of empires are aspects of it. Today the West uncompromisingly rejects the idea of maintaining order through empire. But this need not mean that each state will corrupt its liberty into licence as it pursues its own interests in total disregard of international wellbeing. It is true, as Bishop Berkeley said,[58] that westward the course of empire takes its way; but with the setting of the sun, there is also the promise of the morrow's dawn.

In fact tomorrow's dawn may be already breaking. New political ideas and novel combinations are in the air, containing within them perhaps the secret of how to combine national liberty with supranational order. The Europe of the nine is not just another of the military alliances of which history knows so many; and it is not just one more empire in which national identities have become submerged. Nor can so heterogeneous a collection of states be thought of as a federal union. The Europe of the nine is an association of states that have agreed to subordinate unfettered sovereignty to mutual welfare. There is freedom of trade and, much more important, freedom of migration between them; and they seek to offer full scope to individual enterprise and creativity. Linked moreover through Britain and France with the more amorphous associations of states left over from yesterday's empires, the nine present some kind of world-wide look.

Where all this will lead no one can foretell. History has no more business with the yet-to-be than with the might-have-been. Hypothetical history is not a worth-while exercise and can lead only to doubtful prophecies about the future: as one knows, *l'avenir est à Dieu . . . le passé est à l'histoire*. But from its study of the past history does derive reassurance as well as information. It is the past that encourages our hopes for the challenge of the future.

Notes

1. The treaty establishing the Irish Free State.
2. See, for instance, C. Barnett, *The Collapse of British Power* (London: Eyre Methuen, 1972); and especially P. A. Brunt, 'Reflections on British and Roman Imperialism' in *Comparative Studies in Society and History*, 7 (1965), pp. 267–88.
3. H. A. L. Fisher, *A History of Europe* (London: Edward Arnold & Co., 1936), p. v.
4. For the Roman Empire in the days of the Roman Republic see E. Badian, *Roman Imperialism in the Late Republic* (Pretoria, 1967) and *Publicans and Sinners* (Ithaca, N.Y.: Cornell University Press, 1972), *passim*.
5. Virgil, *Aeneid*, 6. 851–3.
6. See, for example, Pliny, *H.N.*, *Praef.* 16.
7. Tacitus, *Histories*, 4. 72–4.
8. Sir John Seeley, *The Expansion of England* (London: Macmillan, 1883), p. 8.
9. Adam Smith, *The Wealth of Nations* (London: Dent, 1929), p. 408.
10. Plutarch, *Gaius Gracchus*, 2. 10; Aulus Gellius, 15. 12. 4.
11. Dio Cassius, 56. 16. 3.
12. Cicero, *pro lege Manilia*, 65.
13. See, for instance, Cicero, *pro lege Manilia*, 38.

14. T. Drew-Bear in *Historia*, 21 (1972), p. 81.

15. Livy, 45, 18. 3; 45. 29. 11; Diodorus, 31. 8. 7.

16. The most forceful expression of this attitude is probably to be found in J. A. Hobson, *Imperialism: a Study* (London: Allen & Unwin, 1902).

17. Thucydides, 1. 75. 76.

18. Cicero, *de officiis*, 1. 38.

19. J. d'Ormesson, *La Gloire de l'Empire* (Paris: Gallimard, 1971).

20. W. Dittenberger, *Sylloge Inscriptionum Graecarum*, 2⁴. no. 543, p. 20.

21. Pliny, *H.N.*, 9. 117.

22. S. L. Dyson in *Historia*, 20 (1971), pp. 239–74.

23. Dio Cassius, 56. 33. 3.

24. B. Dobson in *Recherches sur les structures sociales dans l'antiquité classique* (Paris: C.N.R.S., 1970), pp. 99–116.

25. Dio Cassius, 79. 20. 3.

26. See A. R. Birley, *Septimius Severus* (London: Eyre & Spottiswoode, 1971), *passim*.

27. Sir Ronald Syme, *Colonial Élites* (London: Oxford University Press, 1958) (Whidden Lectures, Series 3).

28. Cf. Tacitus, *Annals*, 16. 27.

29. See R. MacMullen in *Historia*, 14 (1965), pp. 85f.

30. F. W. Walbank in *Harvard Studies in Classical Philology*, 76 (1972), pp. 145–68.

31. Dio Cassius, 78. 13. 2f.; Flüss in *Realencyclopädie der Alterumswissenschaft*, 14 (1930), s.v. 'Marcius, no. 34', cols. 1547–9.

32. E. Gibbon, *The Decline and Fall of the Roman Empire* (4th

edition, edited by J. B. Bury. London: Methuen, 1906), 1, p. 78.

33. See C. P. Jones, *Plutarch and Rome* (Oxford: Clarendon Press, 1971), *passim.*

34. For example, Sarmatae in A.D. 333.

35. J. Robert Oppenheimer in conversation with the author in 1962.

36. See E. Grierson, *The Imperial Dream* (London: Collins, 1972).

37. *Memorandum Relating to Indians in Kenya* (Command Paper 1922 of H.M. Government, 1923), p. 10.

38. W. R. Crocker, *On Governing Colonies* (London: Allen & Unwin, 1947), p. 139.

39. See, for example, G. Leclerc, *Anthropologie et Colonialisme* (Paris: Fayard, 1971), *passim.*

40. Note the prescient remarks of Tacitus, *Annals*, 1. 4.

41. Cicero, *de legibus*, 3. 18; Tacitus, *Annals*, 15. 21. 1.

42. See R. K. Sherk in *Historia*, 20 (1971), pp. 110–21.

43. G. M. Bersanetti, *Studi sull'imperatore Massimino il Trace* (Rome, 1940), p. 17.

44. Plutarch, *de tranquillitate animi*, 470c.

45. See J. Bayet, *Croyances et rites dans la Rome antique* (Paris: Payot, 1971), *passim.*

46. See the Feriale Duranum published by R. O. Fink, A. S. Hoey, and W. F. Snyder in *Yale Classical Studies*, 7 (1940).

47. R. MacMullen, *Enemies of the Roman Order* (Cambridge, Mass.: Harvard University Press, 1966), pp. 95–127.

48. See A. Magdelain, 'Auspicia ad patres redeunt' in

Hommages à Jean Bayet (Brussels: Collection Latomus, 1964), pp. 427–73.

49. Carus in 283 is the earliest example: Aurelius Victor, *Caesares*, 37. 5; Mommsen, *Römisches Staatsrecht*, 2^3, p. 843.

50. A. H. M. Jones, *Constantine and the Conversion of Europe* (Harmondsworth: Penguin Books, 1972), pp. 96–105.

51. See P. Brown, *The World of Late Antiquity* (London: Thames & Hudson, 1971) and *Religion and Society in the Age of Saint Augustine* (London: Faber & Faber, 1972).

52. A. D. Nock in *Harvard Theological Review*, 23 (1930), pp. 256–60.

53. Tacitus, *Annals*, 15. 31.

54. See Tacitus, *Histories*, 4. 14.

55. See, for instance, such works as A. P. Thornton, *The Imperial Idea and its Enemies* (London: Macmillan, 1959), and J. D. B. Miller, *Britain and the Old Dominions* (London: Chatto & Windus, 1966).

56. J. E. Wrench, *Alfred Lord Milner* (London: Eyre & Spottiswoode, 1958), p. 229.

57. In conformity with this doctrine, British capital was just as likely to be invested in, and British imports to be obtained from, non-Empire countries. Conversely, foreign countries were freely permitted to exploit the resources of Empire countries.

58. Over two hundred years ago in his poem, *On the Prospects of Planting Arts and Learning in America*.